**Praise for *Ar***

*Jan Groft writes with the assurance of one who has known
what it is to suffer loss and abide in the darkness.
In* Artichokes & City Chicken, *she takes the reader one step
beyond into the territory of grace and mercy.*

—Deborah Stewart, author of *Where the Heart Is*

*This is what I call a comfy book...I feel embraced by Jan's story
and helped by her insight, as though, in reading her chapters,
I've spent time with a spiritual companion on a common journey.*

—Vinita Hampton Wright, author of *The Art of Spiritual
Writing* and *Days of Deepening Friendship*

*Groft writes of shedding her self-protective armor
to embrace life the way it should be lived, with a wide-open heart
and her internal chatter stilled to the point that she can almost
hear God breathing.*

—P. J. Lazos, author of *Six Sisters, a collection of novellas*

**Praise for *As We Grieve***

*Jan Groft has written a winner. These are true stories
of heavy hearts, which somehow, through faith, find a way
to keep beating with joy.*

—Barbara Cloud, *Pittsburgh Post Gazette* Columnist
and author of *By-Line*

*Reading* As We Grieve *is like having a support group on paper.*

—*Lancaster Sunday News*

*Touching, painfully honest and soul-cleansing,*
As We Grieve *opens doors of healing, helping to find meaning in life's significant losses.*

—Noah Martin, D. Min., author of *Tears in a Bottle:*
*Comfort for Life's Pain*

As We Grieve *is a book of marvelous depth . . .*
*It is about listening to a still small voice, experiencing God's presence and encountering incredible grace.*

—Tom Dodge, BCC, Director of Spiritual Care,
Hospice of Lancaster County

*With articulate candor, sensitivity, grace,*
*and deep spiritual wisdom . . .* As We Grieve *is a tender*
*treasure for the journey of life.*

—The Rt. Rev. Nathan D. Baxter, Episcopal Bishop of Central
Pennsylvania and former Dean of the National Cathedral

## Praise for *Riding the Dog*

*Jan Groft speaks through every page of this warm-hearted and moving memoir with candor, humility and an abundance of grace. Full of wonder and hard-won wisdom about letting go and letting faith guide the process, Groft's story is, above all, about the gifts of love in its many forms.*

—Ellen Lesser, author of *The Blue Streak*
and *The Shoplifter's Apprentice*

# artichokes
# & city chicken

*Reflections on Faith, Grief,*
*and My Mother's Italian Cooking*

# artichokes & city chicken

jan groft

RIVER GROVE
BOOKS

This is a work of creative nonfiction. The events are portrayed to the best of the author's memory. While all the stories in this book are true, some names and identifying details may have been changed to protect the privacy of the people involved.

Published by River Grove Books
Austin, TX
www.rivergrovebooks.com

Distributed by River Grove Books

Design and composition by Groft Design
Cover design by Groft Design
Cover image: © istockphoto.com/molucas-green-watercolour by kentarcajuan
Cover image: © istockphoto.com/artichoke-vintage-illustration by Oliver Hoffmann
Inside image: © istockphoto.com/retro photo border by jamessnazell

Portions of this book previously appeared in *Central PA Magazine,* published by WITF, Inc. and *Sunday News,* published by Lancaster Newspapers, Inc.

All Scripture quotations, unless otherwise indicated, are taken from the Holy Bible, New International Version®, NIV®. Copyright ©1973, 1978, 1984, 2011 by Biblica, Inc.™ Used by permission of Zondervan. All rights reserved worldwide. www.zondervan.com The "NIV" and "New International Version" are trademarks registered in the United States Patent and Trademark Office by Biblica, Inc.™

Cataloging-in-Publication data is available.

Print ISBN: 978-1-63299-066-2

eBook ISBN: 978-1-63299-067-9

First Edition

For my family

# contents

*Let the water soothe your soul.*

*Let the water take you places,*

*places you could never imagine.*

*Let the water guide you.*

*God is the water.*

—Katherine Groft, age 10

# *preface*

*Nothing ever goes away until it has taught us what we need to know.*
—Pema Chödrön

My quest to decipher a sacred voice—a soothing elixir to heartache—was unknowingly provoked by one long deceased. Hearing was not her strong suit; in fact, she was nearly deaf with precious little function in her right ear only. God has a way of choosing the most unlikely among us to perform certain feats.

It all started in the early 1920s, in Hayes, Pennsylvania, three decades before I was born. The little girl, Giuseppina, stands on the stoop of her family's home, a gray splintered shack, paint peeling. A ripped screen door is slapped on the front like a Band-Aid. Voices rise from the kitchen in back; mason jars clink against porcelain. Giuseppina's sisters and brothers fill every space: Annunziata, Theresa, Rosie, Regina, Felice, Vincenzo. The girls are canning tomatoes, the stink as putrid as dead rats. One, with arms frosted in soapsuds to the elbows, barks at another to get her face away from the washboard. The boys roughhouse until their father displays a clenched fist, sending them running to their chores, pulling onions and hoeing dirt in the garden.

Giuseppina—Pippi for short, meaning "little one"—is the youngest. Her hair is straight, the color of a fawn, her eyes hazel, her sweater threadbare. She waits, clutching a brown paper bag worn from repeated use. Inside is the sum of her possessions: a shiny stone found behind the outhouse, a tattered holy card featuring the Blessed Virgin Mary, a frayed nightshirt and overalls, handed down, as is the dress that hangs on her. The makeshift satchel also holds a loaf of bread, baked in the outdoor brick oven, and tomatoes harvested from the garden.

Her immigrant mother is tiny with a tightly pulled bun, chattering in Italian about Pippi's visit to Giastina's house. She says that it will be an adventure and reminds her daughter to do what is asked of her. She does not mention a date of return, if indeed there is one. The oldest sister, Giastina, whose nickname is Jay, is married to a streetcar driver. The little one has never been away from her mama and papa or the other sisters and brothers. She looks down at her scuffed brown shoes, uncertain and confused.

The picture rendered here is more of a painting than a photograph, imbued with details that may or may not be accurate. Giuseppina, or Pippi, was my mother—Josephine, in English. She has been gone for years now, but it was not her death that separated us. There had always been a failed connection. I imagine that the difficulties between us took root that day long ago when she was sent away from home. I am still processing it all; sometimes it takes a long time.

I knew nothing of Mother's abandonment until she was ninety years old. She mentioned it matter-of-factly one day, when I was visiting at her retirement community. She sat on a khaki-colored loveseat against the wall on which I'd hung two botanical prints in dark bamboo frames. I was sipping tea in the wing chair nearby, which was tilted slightly toward her. Because of her hearing deficiency, and now the dementia, it was nearly impossible to hold conversations of any substance with her. I forget what she'd been talking about the moment she dropped in a reference to the time that she was sent to live with her oldest sister. I looked up from my cup.

"You lived with Aunt Jay?" I asked.

"What?"

"Did you say that you lived with Aunt Jay?"

She nodded.

"Why?"

"What?" She fiddled with her hearing aid.

"Why? Why did you live with Aunt Jay?"

She shrugged, "I guess there were too many of us kids or something."

"When?"

"Huh?"

"How old were you?"

"How old was I?"

"Yes. How old?"

"I don't know," she said. "Maybe seven, eight."

I asked what it was like living there. When she finally deciphered my question, she answered simply, "Nice." But what I would come to wonder and did not ask was this: How did she feel about moving away from home? Who told her about it, and what did they say? Not that she would have acknowledged any hardship. Her secrets were well guarded, and because she typically brushed away questions, I hesitated to intrude. She rarely spoke of her youth, and when she did, her comments were brief, and then she would change the subject.

"Jay bought me my first pair of dress shoes," she added. A detail! Oh, how I craved them! "Black and white patent leather. High-tops."

"How long did you live with her?" Again, the question had to be repeated.

"When her daughter was born—the first one, Lena—there wasn't room for me. They only had a little place, so I was sent back home."

"Severe separations in early life," writes author Judith Viorst, "leave emotional scars on the brain because they assault the essential human connection: the mother-child bond, which teaches us that we are lovable. The mother-child bond, which teaches us how to love."[1]

Later, in fifth or eighth grade—I've heard it both ways—Pippi has to leave school to help at home, or maybe it was because the streetcar fare was unaffordable. Again, the facts are hazy.

According to Viorst, "When separation imperils that early attachment, it is difficult to build confidence, to build trust, to acquire the conviction that throughout the course of our life we will—and deserve to—find others to meet our needs."

At age eighteen, when a self-assured Italian boy leads her over the West Virginia border to elope, she has no concept of the dreams to which he will someday aspire—a thriving business, banquets over which he'll preside and at which her presence, in formal regalia, will be required. He would also have a propensity for inviting guests to their dinner table, from the lowliest of orphans to President Eisenhower's Army Chief of Staff, a neighbor whose circular driveway and stone-pillared home are concealed behind a massive wall of magnolias.

I was a child when Dad extended the invitation to General Matthew B. Ridgway and his family, so the general's status meant nothing to me. It would be years before I discovered his name in my high school history book, an "unflamboyant officer" who succeeded General Douglas MacArthur, leading US forces in Normandy and United Nations troops in Korea. At our dining room table, General Ridgway made pleasant conversation, as did his wife, who appeared regal and polished, dark hair swept high with what looked like a chopstick poking through it. Their son, Matty, was my age, a miniature replica of his father—though not bald—garbed in blazer and tie, nibbling at his potatoes, expressionless.

The evening's accoutrements, compared to our family's customary style of entertaining, seemed curiously incongruous: the absence of Mother's Italian cuisine (we were eating American), the company of strangers in a home typically brimming with relatives, and the presence of Adele, our housecleaner, swishing through the swinging door from the kitchen, carrying and serving the evening's fare.

Earlier, when I'd asked why Adele was there and why she was wearing a maid's costume, Mother's nostrils had flared, and she ordered me to keep quiet; the event, it was clear, was all Dad's doing. Mother would never have relinquished the kitchen—her comfort spot—of her own accord, but on this particular evening, she sat in the formal dining room as though a guest herself, nails painted glossy red, hands wringing the napkin on her lap. This world, it seems, was one that Mother had entered with the same passivity with which, as a child, she went to live with her sister. It was as foreign to her as the Taj Mahal.

Though the experiences of childhood loss may not be consciously remembered in detail, Viorst suggests that we retain "what it surely must have felt like to be powerless and needy and alone." And so there is an expectation of abandonment, of betrayal, of refusal, of disappointment. "Fearful of separation, we establish . . . anxious and angry attachments."[2]

I begin here not because I intend to write my mother's story—it would flounder from gaping holes and mere speculation—but because when the Spirit moved me to open a black box where a tiny but forgotten memory of her awaited (about which you will soon read), I think there was a reason for this nudge. My mother's heartache, as much as she tried to suppress it, is buried in me, as well.

The world in which we find ourselves can seem like an ill-fitting shirt, too stiff or too loose. We feel lost in it, drowning, or poured in tight as a sausage. We are blindsided by worry. We hit rough patches with people close to us. We feel rejected, scattered like litter on a city street. Like the character Ezra in Anne Tyler's novel *Dinner at the Homesick Restaurant*, we harbor reticence.

"I'm worried if I come too close, they'll say I'm over-stepping. They'll say I'm pushy or . . . emotional," he says. "But if I back off, they might think I don't care. I really, honestly believe I missed some rule that everyone else takes for granted; I must have been absent from school that day. There's this narrow little dividing line I somehow never located."[3]

For anyone who has ever yearned to belong, to feel understood, to find harmony or wholeness or peace, this book is for you, as surely as it is for Mother and me. Offered in the spirit of exploration, it is an attempt to connect with the life-giving force that guides us through valleys. Faith is the light by which I find hope and healing. For the seeker in all of us, the question persists: How can we decipher the voice that knows which path to take, the voice that comforts as we try to find our way, the voice that holds us up with love?

Each of our journeys is sure to be unique in hundreds of ways, but perhaps we are all like the woman in the Gospel of Matthew who has been hemorrhaging for years, wending through the crowd, trying to touch the robe of Jesus. That blessed and sacred communion—the moment of healing—is what I see at the root of our deepest yearning.

J.G.

# My Mother's Orange Salad

Hot pepper
Oil (1 tablespoon to each orange)
Black pepper
One orange per person
Salt

For my mother, food was love. The recipes she left behind often fail to provide specifics. We can take that as an opportunity to exercise individuality, to add spices in measures that satisfy our own tastes. But if you must have details, I remember that she peeled and sectioned the oranges and used a very light sprinkling of red pepper flakes (or, in her words, "hot pepper"). I honestly don't recall whether she used olive oil or vegetable oil, so you are on your own with that one.

Chapter One

# if a tree falls in the forest

*God's silences are actually his answers.*
—Oswald Chambers

It has been three months now, and I am still lost. Anything I have ever known about writing seems to have evaporated. Absent, gone. Nonexistent. It is worse than constipation. I try pushing through it, not counting the three-hour breakfasts with a neighbor, the Zumba lessons, the week spent organizing recipes. Pencil markings on paper, hands folded in prayer, teacup stains on a desk bearing elbows, hands holding head. Still, nothing.

It makes me wonder. Who am I and where did I come from and what am I doing here on Earth, other than devouring dark russet potato chips?

Do I even have a voice?

This subject of hearing, of being heard, has been prominent throughout my life. I could talk, I could shout, I could sing, and chances were that my mother, severely impaired by Ménière's Disease, would not hear me. Or, if she did, that which was heard may not have matched that which was intended. Yet it was more than the physical ailment that stymied connection. With a swat of her hand through the air, she'd dismiss my words as though they were pestering flies or turn her back on me, endlessly stirring sauce simmering on the stove. Or, unable to recognize my voice, she'd slam down the phone when I called, the silence between us impenetrable. The old philosophical query comes to mind: If a tree falls in the forest and no one is around to hear it, does it make a sound?

Now the writing, which I nursed and rocked and held close to me, has gone silent. The separation gnaws at me. It is true that I've been among those pooh-poohing the idea of writer's block, an annoying just-do-it type, but now the frantic search for a topic leads me to a small black box perched on my study bookshelf—the one labeled "Ideas." It is the repository for a mishmash of ponderings that I someday might tackle on the page. This is the first time that I am lifting the lid in the hope of finding—versus depositing—a nugget of inspiration.

There in the box is an index card. It is dated August 3, 2006, and contains these notes:

*Mother moved to Structured Living.*[4]

*"My Mother's Clock" (possible essay title)*

*Mother's clock is off by four and a half hours. This is nothing new. In the past, the timepiece has been wrong by six, eight, even ten hours, slowly losing time, but she has refused to adjust it. It is a Sonic Boom model purchased for its thundering alarm to compensate for her hearing loss. Across the side buttons, she has taped a sliver of a Band-Aid to keep my sister and me from fiddling with the settings.*

I barely remember capturing these thoughts on paper, but I do recall the clock, the way it lost time, and that Mother wouldn't allow us to reset it or change the batteries for fear of breaking it. (We did these things only when we could sneak them past her.) Dementia had set in, possibly confusing the essence of time, and compounding what had already been distorted reasoning, distrust and suspicions, agitation and anxiety. In addition, she had been deaf in the left ear for as long as I could remember.

"Nobody tells me anything!" she would snap.

The feelings of isolation emanated, in part, from this impaired hearing. It is also true that I, for one, was reticent to open up to her. The recurring negativity felt like stabs: *Get away from me.* Looking back, I see how unequipped I was— and, finally, too calloused—to understand that the anger and snide remarks were billboards for pain.

After Dad died and we moved Mother north from Florida to care for her, it was like discovering a bundle on the doorstep, foreign, unknowable, as my sisters and I groped through the webs of dementia and hearing loss, now affecting her right ear, as well. She was eighty-six, and she lived until age ninety-two.

On the back of the index card: a conversation between Mother and me. We'd been sitting in her room, she on the loveseat and me on a nearby chair. Most likely I'd recorded it to illustrate the mounting difficulty she and I were encountering in our never-ending effort to communicate.

*Me: Did I tell you our cat died?*
*Mother: What?*

*Me: Did I tell you our cat died?*
*Mother: What?*
*Me: OUR CAT DIED!*
*Mother: DO WHATEVER YOU WANT!*

The exchange occurred some time after the heartbreak around the veterinary table as my husband, younger daughter, and I witnessed Murphy's lethal injection, half-blinded by an avalanche of tears. I'd hesitated to mention this sooner to Mother, knowing the challenges of explaining it, not only because of the barrier imposed by the hearing limitations but also because of the fear of her response. Neither of us had mastered the skill of tending emotionally to the other, a reality that made grief even lonelier. When my best friend died at age forty-one, and I shared the excruciating news, Mother had shrugged, "Oh, well, what are you going to do?"

On one level, I was able to acknowledge that her reaction was nothing personal. It's just who she was, addressing the nuisance of pain by refusing to acknowledge it. On another level, I longed for even a tiny sign that she felt my sadness, a hug or some small inflection of voice.

At the time that I jotted the notes on the index card, I had no idea that in less than three weeks, Mother would fall, break her hip, and rush toward death as efficiently as she used to sweep dust from our breezeway floor. The sonic boom clock had slowed down in much the same way that my mother's heart would soon stop beating.

The card triggers memories, and the scribbling takes off: the reprimands over mumbling "just like your father," the slap at the air to dismiss words that were unintelligible to her. And then, the dementia. It arrived like an uninvited guest, illuminating our failure to connect and slamming the door behind itself.

Words spill onto paper, the pangs receding. Breathe, breathe. The page is my harbor. I write and write, and like an image developing through darkroom chemicals, there she is, locked in silence, watching lips move, wondering *are they talking about me?* The distance that existed between us sharpens in focus, not in a way that explains it, but in a way that shines with the indisputable fact that it was not intentional.

My grasp tightens on the pencil, and there is a glimmer of hope: My mother no more wanted to shut me out than she wanted to feel disregarded. Could this struggle to hear my own voice spark the mercy, at last, that might connect us? The thoughts form words; the words lead to an essay; the essay becomes a submission; the submission is rejected. After rereading, I concur that a rejection was deserved. The effort is incomplete, as is my knowledge of the mysteries that were buried in the coffin with Mother, unanswered questions about which I am unable to speculate, hurts that were rooted so deeply in her heart that they led to criticism, bouts of agitation. And yet, at the same time, she was compelled to slough off pain as though it were inconsequential. Finally, I file the piece in a folder labeled "My Mother's Clock."

The attempt, I see now, was a crucial step, an unleashing of sorts. Even more significant was the filing away of it. The letting go. The respite from striving to be heard. Still, the yearning does not go away, for now here it is again—the wrestling with nothingness, a page that is every bit as blank as Mother's expression when I tried and tried to make her hear me. Does God separate me from my words because forcing silence is the only way to penetrate this stubborn skull of mine?

*Zip it!* is what I begin to hear. *I want you to listen.*

To listen?

"When you cannot hear God," writes Oswald Chambers, "you will find that He has trusted you in the most intimate way possible—with absolute silence . . . because He saw that you could withstand an even bigger revelation."[5]

A light flickers, a message illuminated. The silence. The longing for closeness.

"We have run away from most of our pain for so long," writes Stephen Levine, "that we now have no idea how to deal with it."[6] With Mother long gone, I wonder if bridging the gap left behind is still a possibility. I want to believe that it is, and that she has been resurrected through grace by a God who is master of second and third and hundredth, no, infinite chances.

At times, our hearts feel so shattered, our brains so distraught, that we question whether God is anywhere in the neighborhood. We might even feel irked, believing, as Mary and Martha did, that Jesus is dillydallying elsewhere, while our own needs for help are profound.

When their brother, Lazarus, fell sick and died, both women complained, "Lord, if you had been here, my brother would not have died."[7]

The parable of Lazarus encourages faith in a higher power, even when trust appears to arrive too late. With God, it is never too late. And so Jesus commands those surrounding Lazarus's tomb to take away the stone.

Ugh, Martha insists. It's been four days since he died. The odor will be preposterous.

"Did I not tell you," says Jesus, "that if you believed, you would see the glory of God?"[8]

As Lazarus walks out of the tomb, with hands and face and feet still wrapped in burial linens, the glory of God is nearly blinding. It's a promise we've heard again and again: *Nothing is impossible with God.* Resolution can be found even after years of unforgiveness. Reconciliation can occur even after death slams the door. Hurts can heal. Peace can arrive. *Nothing is impossible with God.*

The same heart that holds hurt, aching and broken, can also be the vehicle for healing. For it is through the heart that we listen. It is right there in black and white: the word "ear" tucked into "hear," both cradled into "heart."

They say that to *show* love, one must *feel* loved. Does this mean that to hear, the heart must first feel heard?

I think of my father's mantra, staunchly delivered: *Think positive! Mind over matter!* As a literal-minded kid, I began shelving negative feelings in deference to my father's unflinching brand of optimism that appeared to conquer all. By over-subscribing to this philosophy, I succeeded in some ways. At the same time, I learned to disregard a small, hurting voice: my own.

Yet even Jesus got angry (remember how he flipped over the merchants' tables outside the tabernacle?) and sad ("Jesus wept" at the sight of his friend Lazarus's lifeless body[9]) and desperate ("My God, my God, why have you forsaken me?"[10]). Nobody ever called Jesus a whiner. It seems telling that the man for whom God's voice was most audible was deeply in touch with his own heart's bidding.

After years of practice, my adeptness at tuning out the negative grew. It is not easy granting ample airtime to sorrow, when one's tendency has been to head up the search team for the silver lining. A positive attitude can be a handy asset; don't get me wrong. Gratitude and hope are the makings of a life filled with joy. But in addition to the Norman Vincent Peale books and Dale Carnegie lectures, perhaps our hearts could use some listening lessons.

Can a person *learn* to listen? Grow in it?

God promised that if we listen and try to understand, if we seek out insight as we would hidden treasure, we'll find knowledge and wisdom, protection. We'll understand what's right and what path to take.

"For wisdom will enter your heart,
  and knowledge will be pleasant to your soul.
Discretion will protect you,
  and understanding will guard you."[11]

When I was a college freshman, I struggled with a music appreciation course. The professor, Truman Bullard, was a renowned maestro, balding and compact. His passion for the classics energized the classroom. With grandiose gestures and a boom box on his desk, he brought them alive—Gregorian chants, symphonies, opera—like an orchestra conductor coaxing out the woodwinds. In spite of Dr. Bullard's efforts and my long hours wearing headphones to study in the library, I was lost. The music was lovely, but remembering and identifying which composer scored which piece seemed beyond comprehension. I was failing the course.

Then, during Christmas break while I was at home, it just so happened that the opera to be covered on our final exam, *Don Giovanni,* was scheduled to appear on public television. I was glued to the set. By *seeing* the characters, I came to know them and the pieces they performed. With the addition of the visual dimension, I was able to *hear.* In the end, I aced the test, catapulting my grade to a more respectable level.

The One who created us knows that we each have our own unique way of hearing and is more than willing to oblige. All it takes, God promises, is faith as tiny as a mustard seed. Not a whole crop of it, not even the sprout, just one tiny seed. So faith, as infinitesimal as it may be, comes first. In the words of St. Anselm of Canterbury, "I do not seek to understand so that I can believe, but I believe so that I may understand."

Author Catherine Marshall writes of how the Bible underwent a transformation for her once she committed her life to God.

"The more I read in this remarkable book," she asserts,

"the more surely I knew that in its pages God Himself was speaking to me." The affirmation—the ability to hear and recognize a divine voice—springs from faith itself.

"We arrive at surety by one of two routes," she notes. "With questions pertaining to our bodies or material matters, we are convinced by intellectual, scientific or evidential proof. With questions pertaining to man's spirit, we are convinced only by personal revelation. For instance, a question like 'How do I know He loves me?' can never be proved by reasoning or in the laboratory. For love is in the area of spirit from whose door the scientific kind of proof is turned away every time. Yet the flooding inner revelation: 'He *does* love me! He loves *me!*' is valid, bringing such surety that I am willing to commit my life to my love."[12]

Yes, the flooding inner revelation. The grace that rises from loss, the trials that instruct, the overwhelming encounters with nature. Can it be that receiving divine love means standing before God even in our ugliest, sorriest, saddest moments, and opening up to revelation? Even as unpracticed in receiving as we may be?

The flooding arrives in the quiet or amid crowds, in times of prayer or deep sorrow, in the beckoning hours of awakening or the weighty moments before sleep, in the crusty fields of farms or the soul-cleansing warmth of the rain shower, on drives through the countryside or across the interstate. It can also be triggered by the printed word, most notably, as Marshall conveys, on the pages of the Bible.

At a time when I was concerned that the manuscript for my first book, a spiritual memoir, would make its permanent home in a file drawer, a scriptural verse prompted me to reconsider. Propped against pillows in a hotel room bed after a grueling day at a writers' conference, I encountered the words. The publisher I'd met with that afternoon advised that the time wasn't right for getting a memoir to print; various workshop leaders concurred. These were the experts; they knew the state of the industry and, according to them, regardless of writing quality, the climate was such that publishing houses were not willing to invest in autobiographical material written by high-risk (a.k.a. unknown) authors.

Years of crafting the manuscript tumbled free fall through my mind. I wanted to catch and save it somehow, but I felt powerless, uninitiated. *Riding the Dog* had been my first major effort at spiritual writing. My own experience of flooding inner revelation had inspired it: an unmistakable holy presence during a summer of intense grief. Now, in the hotel bed with a Bible resting on my lap, I randomly turned to a page. And there, a verse, which did not seem random at all, awaited: "I am the voice of one calling in the wilderness, 'Make straight the way for the Lord.'"[13]

The words made a beeline for my heart. I read them again. It was true. I am just one voice, a small one, to be sure, and isn't every single one of us just one voice? A renewed determination stirred within me to use my God-given talent in a way that felt right. It wasn't easy, but within six months, the book was under contract for publication.

How does this stirring arise? From where does it emanate? I think it goes something like this: The minute we believe, even in a tiny-mustard-seed-size proportion, the voice of the Holy Spirit stirs within. It encourages and inspires with no other motive than to help us become who God created us to be. Peace-filled, profound, tenacious, and true, it arrives in our hearts like a holy whisper.

Long ago, a sign was posted along the Pennsylvania Turnpike in areas that were under construction. On the sign was an illustration of a white-bearded man wearing a red, white, and blue top hat, apparently "Uncle Sam," pointing his forefinger at passersby. The words in capital letters accompanying the drawing were: "YOU, SLOW DOWN." I am typically not a shouting person, nor do I respond well to those who shout at me. My reaction to this sign was visceral. Whenever I saw it, my inclination was to step on the gas.

The sign was the antithesis of the tender voice that we know as that of the Holy Spirit—unassuming, meshing seamlessly with our own instincts. In a pitch akin to that of intuition, it is not pushy, and it doesn't yell.

In *The Writer's Survival Guide*, author Rachel Simon addresses the topic of inner voice. Her comments are directed to writers, but they also ring true for other vocations— parent, artist, accountant, teacher, nurse—whose names can be substituted in the brackets I've added. She warns that "the inner voice is, at least initially, rather shy, and if a [writer] isn't careful, he might ignore it."

Simon makes a relevant distinction between fear and the inner voice. "Fear screams," she notes, "while the inner voice whispers. Fear throws manipulative, negative-thought temper tantrums, while the inner voice prods gently. Fear seems thunderous, paralyzing. It demands we stop. It wants to shackle our hands, rip us out of the process, make us prove to ourselves that we are no good at [writing] and, consequently, at anything. . . . The inner voice is patient. It knows it will keep nagging you until you act, and so it lets you go on until you act. . . . The inner voice cajoles and suggests and waits until you get around to paying attention."[14]

Likewise, author and pastor Max Lucado contrasts the aggressive way of the world with the gentleness of the Lord. "The world rams at your door; Jesus taps at your door," he writes. "The voices scream for your allegiance; Jesus softly and tenderly requests it. The world promises flashy pleasure; Jesus promises a quiet dinner . . . with God."[15]

My friend Maxine explains it simply: "God puts thoughts in our minds. Then the thought just won't go away. It keeps coming back, and that's God impressing on you what to do."

My friend Mildred contends that the voice of the Holy Spirit "says what it has to say plainly and clearly and with authority. It doesn't elaborate."

In describing Jesus, the apostle John writes that "his voice was like the sound of rushing waters"[16]—a steady, soothing, and sure presence.

In a mysterious mingling of the human and the divine, the inner spirit guides. Precious gift, tender, worthy of attention. *Yes, try this way*, it suggests. Or it arrives in the form of an idea under construction (*I wonder what would*

*happen if . . .*), empowering our instincts. There is no judging, no forcing, simply the sacred aura of possibility.

The other voice, the one of fear, as Simon notes, jumps to conclusions. *Nah, not me. That would never work.* Its tones are negative; it uses absolutes like *never* and *can't.* It puts a damper on exploration that has not even begun. Ah, yes, the knee-jerk reaction.

A pastor who invited me to speak at a church luncheon asked me to talk about my approach to writing books. Specifically, he wanted me to address the topic, "How does faith play a role in your work?" No one had ever asked this question of me. It made me flinch at first: How would I provide a twenty-minute answer that anyone would care about?

In preparing my talk, I learned several truths. First, the question goes straight to the core of what matters. Second, answering it reveals that the process—even though it involves sitting alone at a desk day after day, week after week—is not a solitary one, nor am I even the source of it. Third, by prompting retrospection, the question enhances appreciation for grace, whose essence, I think, is that it picks us up and moves us forward in spite of our cluelessness.

And finally, there is no twenty-minute answer. Twenty minutes was a good start; it opened the floodgates. But even now, the question remains.

How does faith play a role . . . ?

The query might be posed in myriad ways and applied to a variety of circumstances. How does faith play a role in our work, our relationships, our sense of well-being? An exercise of this type—one involving self-exploration—can prompt a journey in listening.

Voice, definition number eight: "a quality that seems to proceed from a will or personality: the voice of nature."[17]

Isaiah writes: "Whether you turn to the right or to the left, your ears will hear a voice behind you, saying, 'This is the way; walk in it.'"[18]

The Psalmist declares that there is no speech or language where the voice of the heavens is not heard.[19]

I remember a car ride one summer, while we were hosting a French student in our home. I can still see sixteen-year-old Clémence in the back seat with Katherine, my own teenage daughter. Tall and model-thin with long, dark hair and rimless glasses, Clémence had been in the United States for two weeks. Her command of our language was better than indicated on the International Cultural Exchange application form; she had rated her English as "poor," but we'd been impressed by it. Still, my husband, my daughter, and I were discussing the energy required to communicate day in and day out in a foreign language. Clémence had another week remaining before returning home.

"Are you looking forward to speaking French again?" I asked.

"A little," Clémence admitted.

"Maybe we can reprogram the navigation system to speak French," Randy offered. He backed into a parking space beside our church. "Not exactly stimulating, but still."

Katherine and I laughed and then immediately latched

onto the idea. It seemed an ingenious way to offer Clémence the comfort of hearing the language that was natural to her. The car owner's manual was in the glove compartment, and I reached for it. As I read, Randy poked keys on the dashboard, noting that the text above the steering wheel had converted to French, but the audible female prompts continued in English.

Finally, the church bells rang, and Randy attempted to exit the system.

"It says something about being a quitter," he noted, attempting to translate the French.

"That's actually pronounced kee-tay," I said, tapping into the minimal remains of long-ago French classes. "It's a verb that means to leave. Just push OK."

After church, we drove north on Queen Street toward home and decided to give the navigation system another try. Randy pulled over to the curb. We would not be quitters.

I began reading from the manual where we'd left off earlier. The system's setup offered the ability to change to a male voice, among other options. There was an asterisk with a note in small print.

"Oh, it says that translations to French and Spanish are currently in development and will be available in the future."

We sighed, disappointed, Clémence, too, who seemed politely amused by our feeble attempt to make her feel at home.

"Well, then, can we change it to a male voice?" Katherine asked.

"No," said Randy. "I don't like taking orders from a male.

I'm already used to taking them from a female."

We all laughed, but it occurs to me now that our offbeat experiment provides a glimpse of God's desire to engage us while we are, according to Scripture, "like foreigners and strangers on Earth,"[20] making our way home. God goes to all lengths to speak in languages that are familiar to us—through nature, circumstance, art, or the voices of others, to name a few.

Having spent the better part of a lifetime trying to connect with a mother who could not hear, I can barely imagine how my Creator—whose words are infinitely more crucial than mine—must long to talk to me, to walk side by side, with me hanging onto each thought. But I turn a deaf ear. I slam down the phone, unable to recognize what sounds like a whisper. I swat away words dangling before me. How can I be insolent when the offer at hand is that of a peaceful heart?

Perhaps we are just wanderers, groping through ambiguity. Who can help us find our way if not the One who created us? The silence on the page taunts me: the disconnection, the memories it conjures. For others, promptings of a different nature may clamor for attention. As we learn to listen deeply, what will be revealed to us? That is where faith comes in.

"Approaching with mercy and loving kindness that which we have always withdrawn from in fear, judgment, doubt, and distrust," notes Steven Levine, "there arises the possibility for the healing of a lifetime."[21]

"Speak, Lord, for your servant is listening."[22]

# My Mother's Meatball Soup

[1 cup] chicken or beef [cut small]
1 cup chopped celery
[1 small head] chopped cabbage
[1 cup] chopped carrots
[1 cup] chopped onion
Small can tomato sauce
[One bunch] steamed endive
[1 cup] chi-chis (a.k.a. chick peas)
[Small package] frozen corn
1 lb. uncooked miniature meatballs [made from
your favorite Italian meatball recipe]

Put chicken or beef into about two quarts water
on stove. Add all ingredients, except chi-chis
and frozen corn, and cook until vegetables
are tender. Add 1 pound uncooked miniature
meatballs, and simmer until cooked. Then add
chi-chis and frozen corn. Heat through, adding
more water as needed. Salt and black pepper
to taste.

This was, and still is, my favorite soup. Some call it Italian Wedding Soup, but my mother had no leaning toward formalities.

Since her recipes rarely specified measurements, I've taken the liberty of adding my own suggestions [in brackets], but please feel free to simply use a handful of this or pinch of that, just as Mother did.

# waiting

*Never run before God gives you direction.*
*Whenever there is doubt, wait. . . .*
*When God brings a time of waiting, don't fill it*
*with busyness, just wait.*
—Oswald Chambers

It is a crisp autumn day. I pull up across the street from Maxine's house ten minutes early, park along the curb, and turn off the ignition. And there she is, waiting at the side door, her hands folded as though in prayer. She steps outside to greet me, and the sight of her, after all these years, brings tears to my eyes. She looks exactly as I remembered, though two decades have passed since she moved away with her husband, Lee, who is now deceased.

Promptings from two different books have drawn me back to Maxine, who, a long time ago, meticulously cleaned my home when I was a single mother, working to build a business and support my daughter and myself.

The first book, called *Thanks!*, about gratitude and how practicing it can make a person happier, inspired me to make a list of people for whom I've felt grateful. Maxine ranked high. In the second book, *On Caring*, Milton Mayeroff writes about being "in-place." This, he explains, means "to live a life significantly grounded in caring. It is our response to the need of others to grow, which gives us place."[23]

I know many people who live lives significantly grounded in caring, who have followed passions down paths that connect with the growth needs of others—teachers and artists, parents and counselors—but when I read these words, it was Maxine who came to mind. I can still see her squeezing the water from a sponge, detailing a silk tree, leaf by shiny leaf. She emptied ashes and scrubbed the fireplace's charred vanilla bricks, restoring them to the semblance of perfectly aligned teeth that have just had their braces removed. She did these things not because I asked her to—which, quite honestly, never would have occurred to me—but because she elevated the act of housecleaning to the level of sacred praise.

For a single mom trying to make her way in the world, support is a precious commodity. Yet there was something else about Maxine that resonated with me, something bigger than her impeccable work. It was tenderness. The melodic lilt in her voice. The blue-eyed windows to a wide-open soul. The words her presence spoke in me, love-graced. As she walked through the front door of my home, week after week for eight years, a quiet but profound sense of joy came in with her.

One morning, I remember, she showed up glowing with enthusiasm. My daughter and I had just moved from our city row house. Maxine had hardly been able to sleep the night before, she told me, knowing that today she would "get to" clean our new condominium. Her spirit was as cleansing as a house blessing; like her flawless work, it was more than anyone could expect.

Maxine is eighty now, still petite, still wearing a brown curled wig. Her hair began falling out when she gave birth to her second child. She was in the hospital ready to deliver, but the doctor hadn't arrived.

"The doctor that I had, he never wanted to let the nurses deliver a baby unless he was there," she explains. "Well, he wasn't there and he wasn't coming, he wasn't there and wasn't coming. And Judy *was* coming."

So a nurse gave her ether in an effort to calm her.

"Nearly broke my nose," Maxine says, "and, of course, I went to sleep with that ether. They just gave me so much, more than I was supposed to have, I'm sure, but how that happened, I don't know. There were just little pieces of hair all over my pillow and I thought, *What in the world?* So little by little, over the years, my hair kept falling out."

Waiting can be grueling. It can seem impossible, as it must have for Maxine when she was told to wait at the moment of delivery. Thankfully, God continues working miracles even, and especially, through our pain.

"I remember when I got awake," recalls Maxine, "and they said, 'You have a little girl,' and I said, 'Ahhhh, just what I wanted!'"

"Waiting does not diminish us, any more than waiting diminishes a pregnant mother," according to *The Message* Bible translation of Romans 8:25. "We are enlarged in the waiting. We, of course, don't see what is enlarging us. But the longer we wait, the larger we become, and the more joyful our expectancy."[24]

In Genesis, Sarah grew weary of waiting for the offspring that God had promised her and Abraham. Years dragged on, and the couple remained childless. Finally, tired of dashed hopes, Sarah devised a plan of her own: She would have Abraham sleep with her maidservant Hagar, who would bear them a son, Ishmael. Then the impossible happened. At age ninety, Sarah gave birth to Isaac.

Now Sarah's plan paled in comparison to God's plan, the one that had taken so long to unravel. She groused about the idea of her natural son, Isaac, sharing his inheritance with his half-brother, Ishmael. She griped and complained until, finally, Abraham packed up Hagar and Ishmael and sent them away.

When God seems to be taking the scenic route and impatience bears down, it's tempting to scoot into the driver's seat. Heartache and longing, hoping and praying can become wearisome, especially after months or years. It's hard not being privy to God's plans. Waiting to find out can make us feel testy, if not inclined to take over.

In *The Essential Bible Guide,* Whitney Kuniholm addresses the difficulty of letting go of our own ideas and letting God work. The disciples, he points out, needed the Holy Spirit's power to communicate a message.

"But Jesus told them to wait," Kuniholm notes, referring to Acts 1, right before Jesus returned to Heaven. "Sometimes waiting for the Holy Spirit to create an opportunity . . . is difficult. But real results come when we prayerfully wait for a sense of what the Holy Spirit wants us to do."[25]

In the case of the disciples, writes Kuniholm, their waiting led to a "spiritual breakthrough, the unleashing of the Holy Spirit."[26]

In my work, I await the breakthrough and not with much patience. Where is this unleashing of the Holy Spirit? When will it happen? It will be months before I recognize my struggle with writer's block as a manifestation of a deeper yearning for connection. It is not until then, upon looking back, that I will grasp the significance of the memories surfacing and Maxine's role in evoking them.

She sits perpendicular to me on the charcoal velour sectional that, she points out, was chosen by her son, Gary, who lives with her. Her purple turtleneck, purple slacks, white beads, and pink slipper socks bring to mind the colors of Easter, the resurrection.

Years ago, in a note on a Christmas card, Maxine mentioned her diagnosis of Ménière's disease. Immediately, I recognized the name, having known only one other person plagued by it—my mother. It is a disorder of the inner ear that can affect hearing and balance. According to Wikipedia, episodes of vertigo, low-pitched tinnitus, and hearing loss are common with Ménière's. The hearing loss can fluctuate; it comes and goes and finally becomes permanent with no return to normal function.

"It's really a terrible feeling," Maxine says now of the dizzy spells and their unpredictable occurrence. The attacks relegate her to staying indoors while Gary is at work. "It seems like everything I'm looking at just goes round and round real fast, yet inside my head, it goes like this." She bobs her head up and down, up and down. "And then you get real weak, sick in your stomach."

My mother suffered from dizzy spells, though I don't know how long she'd had Ménière's or how she discovered it. She never offered much of an explanation, and I didn't ask. Our relationship was like a dance that never started, both parties failing to make the first move.

The link between Maxine and Mother does not escape me, though at the moment, I have no inkling that the Holy Spirit might be beckoning my return to a relationship presumed ended by death. Maxine describes visits to a Pittsburgh hospital to confirm the diagnosis that her family doctor had already suspected.

"They put me into what looked like a telephone booth, only it was round," she recalls. "It was like being electrocuted. They tied me in there; they tied my feet, and they said, 'Don't move,' and they'd swing it real fast this way, then swing it real fast that way.

"Then another time, they said, 'We're going to blindfold you, but don't shut your eyes.' They blindfolded me, and they swished me around again. Oh, it was really terrible. After-wards, you really felt bad, dizzy."

Finally, Maxine had an operation on her left ear, causing total hearing loss in that ear, as the doctors had predicted it would, but the surgery was necessary to restore balance. Though the dizziness continued on occasion, the tests stopped when there was only three percent hearing remaining in the ear that had not had surgery.

Listening to Maxine's story, I am a little girl again, sitting on Mother's right side in church, or on the bus to downtown Pittsburgh to shop for school clothes. If I sit on the other side, she admonishes, she won't be able to hear me. And then I am older, married with my own children, telephoning my parents, who have moved to Florida. The conversations are essentially between Dad and me. Mother, on an extension line, rarely chimes in and, when she does, her comments indicate a misunderstanding of the topic. She sometimes reports on kidnappings she's read about in the newspaper, extending a warning to watch out for my daughters. When Dad is not home, she sometimes answers the phone, but the connection is limited.

"Hi, Mum!"

"Who is this?"

"It's Jan."

"Who?"

Louder: *"Jan."*

Irritated: *"Who* is it?"

"IT'S JAN! YOUR DAUGHTER!"

"I DON'T KNOW WHAT YOU'RE TALKING ABOUT!" (SLAM)

"For a while I had a regular hearing aid, which I liked," Maxine explains. "Then they said these new ones, the digital, worked better, but it didn't for me. The digital fits *behind* your ear. I'd put my hearing aid on, then my glasses on, and put my wig on. Oh my, it was just terrible. Some can hear better with the digital, but not me. So I got rid of that, and they made me a new one to go *in* my ear."

What is it about Maxine that elicits my compassion? Is it the lilt in her voice, the inviting eyes, the love that emanates from every pore in her body? To be sure, those things are part of it. But I wonder if in hearing Maxine, there is also something different in me, something whose absence opens a passage toward my heart that was clogged in the company of my mother.

Take the issue about the hearing aids. After Dad died, and Mother moved north, I took her to an audiologist, who fitted her with two digital hearing aids to replace the older model she'd worn for years. And for the first time, we began to approach unfettered conversation. But the new push-button technology frustrated her. I didn't know yet that she had dementia and that it is impossible for someone to learn something new when they are in the process of unlearning almost everything they know. Without having the words to explain this, Mother insisted on returning to the original wheel-operated model.

"But you can *hear* us with these!" I protested, my heart sinking at having come so close. Part of the frustration stemmed from an endless desire for connection. The other part, I see now, had more to do with an urgency I felt to repair the untied threads of her spirit.

I may never fully know the roots of my mother's ailments, either physical or emotional, but it was this sense of responsibility for fixing that which was broken in her—and the failure to do so—that is absent in my ability to empathize with Maxine. The truth is that I had no more reign over Mother's well-being than my daughters do over mine. It is a recurrent misgiving: my assumption of responsibility for that over which my control is limited. Perhaps the sliver of Band-Aid with which Mother covered the knobs of her Sonic Boom clock spoke of this very point. It wasn't mine to fix.

Here in Maxine's company, something is stirring within me. The connections provoke memories. There is a resurrection of buried feelings. It seems that years after her death, Mother has joined forces with the Holy Spirit to take my heart where it needs to go.

"… the Lord longs to be gracious to you;
   therefore he will rise up to show you compassion.
For the Lord is a God of justice.
Blessed are all who wait for him!"[27]

Reminders of Mother continue, handed to me tenderly. Maxine describes the indoor regimen that replaces the long walks that she and Lee used to take through the neighborhood. Now with the concern over dizzy spells confining her to the house, she gets exercise by hiking from room to room, one thousand steps; she has counted them out. It is a twenty-minute endeavor that she repeats, often twice a day, carving a path through impediments.

For Mother also, there were treks through the retirement home, where she lived in a first-floor apartment. Outside her door, she would start at one end of the long hallway and snake through the lobby, walk to the other end, up the steps, and through the halls, repeating the pattern floor after floor. As she finished each round, she would leave a scrap of paper on a windowsill to tally the number of trips she had made. Finally, she would clear away the markers, and there would be no hint remaining of the point at which she had started or of the journey that she had endured.

"I never know when it's going to happen and what brings it on. It just comes on." The possibility of dizzy spells is so pressing that Maxine refrains from opening the door to let the family shih tzu out for fear that the dog might run away. Instead, Maggie is trained to relieve herself on waterproof pads near the front door; a note outside directs visitors to enter through the side. "Like when I was in the sunroom. I was just sitting there, feeling great, watching television. I got up and walked to the kitchen door, and it felt like my world turned upside down."

She explains that she stepped back slowly and sat down for a while, and then she walked into the living room, steadying her hands against the wall. She lay down on the sofa. And then she prayed. She waited.

After about half an hour, she recalls, she felt fine. As simple as it may seem, Maxine's wisdom is offered like a feast set at a table where I am the honored guest. Through prayer, she releases her burdens: no demands, no timetable, just genuine belief that a higher power will prevail. She steps back, steadies herself, rests, and prays. Not a bad way to approach the stronghold of pain.

"An assurance and confidence in God in the midst of trials, limitations, past failures and future dangers" produces "the peace, tranquility, and courage of consolation," according to St. Ignatius. This assurance doesn't eliminate the fear, but helps to work through it.[28] Perhaps this is the secret behind Maxine's composure.

From the age of twelve, when she first earned a quarter for cleaning the sunroom of her family's landlady, Maxine held a variety of jobs. One of them was a stint in a nursing home. She knew little about nursing, she admits, and relied on advice from her sister, a nurse. One time, she recalls, a patient had to go to the bathroom. Somehow Maxine, tiny and petite, helped get her to the toilet.

"She was so sick, so bad, and I was on my knees holding her up. She was a big woman. She fell over on me, and she died in my arms."

Maxine shares her stories matter-of-factly, with no particular agenda, but her experiences resonate with me. My effort to care for a mother plagued by multiple difficulties at the end of her life wasn't the last time I would be faced with challenges stretching my capabilities. It happens to all of us. Yet, in spite of unpleasant circumstances, Maxine's actions illuminate the sanctity of holding others up, as heavy as they may seem. I think of Jesus, "full of grace and truth,"[29] demonstrating love and tending to the wounds of others. Who wouldn't want to die in her arms?

Her faith is unwavering; it shines with hope. Is God using Maxine, plagued by impairments of the inner ear, in an effort to help me to hear? Why not? This is the same God who used a man orphaned at birth to part the sea and lead his people to freedom. It is the same Father who crowned a baby born in a manger King of all. I don't yet know where her stories are leading, but in a few days, I feel compelled to call and ask if I may return to record them.

One evening when Maxine attended Minnesota's North Central Bible College, the words "Go teach my gospel" appeared to her in the form of a rainbow. She had gone to the prayer chapel, and after she finished praying, she started to stand, and the vision came to her. She cannot explain it, and she doesn't try to; she just knows that she saw the colorful script encircling the altar. It was an experience she kept to herself over the years, not even sharing it with her future husband. But years after they were married, Lee, who had previously "never had a calling," according to his wife, began to consider leaving his job at the local paper mill to go into ministry. Maxine was hesitant.

*Oh, do we really want to do this?* she thought.

"Well, he was mowing the grass one day with a ride-around lawn mower," she remembers. "He got down to fix something underneath it, but when I looked out the window, I didn't know what had happened. All I could see was his legs and I thought the tractor was on top of him. I said, 'Oh, Lord, I'll do whatever you want me to do. I'll go ahead and go in the ministry with Lee.'

"Sure enough, he got up," she continues. "There was nothing; he was just fixing something underneath, but it was just a way the Lord was talking to me."

Lee and Maxine served various churches throughout

Pennsylvania, he as pastor and she as Sunday school teacher. It was when they arrived at a church in Lancaster that Maxine answered an ad I had placed in the local newspaper for a housecleaner. She took the job to supplement their pastoral income by doing something she'd always loved to do, even as a child.

"You don't like to brag yourself up," she says, smiling. "But Mother would say, 'You're always cleaning!' And Dad would say, 'Now where did Maxine stick that again?' because he'd want a paper or pencil that I'd put away. Everything had to be perfect for me; I just didn't like messy things."

And really, who does like messy things? I think of the Rob Bell book, *Love Wins,* which my Bible study group has been exploring. It tackles the question, "Who gets to go to Heaven?" This ever-constant debate pits Christian against non-Christian and Christians against one another, sparking arguments and igniting wars. The book and the discord that spurred it have been on my mind. While curious about Maxine's perspective, I am secretly fearful that we may be on opposite sides of the fence. But with my friend, as with Jesus, there is no fence; there is only love.

I ask whether she thinks Jews will go to Heaven, and she looks at me as though I have just landed from Mars.

"Jews are God's chosen people!" she defends. I am relieved.

"What about people who have never heard of Jesus Christ, those in Third World countries, for example?"

"The Bible tells us that God is not willing that any should perish," she says.

I mention the disagreement that exists in the interpretation of these words, and she smiles kindly.

"It says right in the Bible: The mysteries belong to God."

Somehow it seems that this is the nugget for which I came. The mysteries belong to God. Maxine acknowledges that a power much higher than she runs the universe. Her very connection to a divine voice emanates, I think, from this handing over of reins, the trust. By abdicating the conflicts, the pontificating, the worry, she is able to wait in faith. Her heart is free to love.

The rainbow of words that Maxine saw, "Go teach my gospel," set the stage for her life's work—teaching the gospel of love—not only as Sunday school teacher but also as a mother, nurse's aide, housecleaner, and friend.

I ask what she thinks it takes to live a fulfilled life. She does not hesitate.

"Everybody wants to be happy," she says. "But to make yourself happy, you have to live to help others."

Her philosophy is affirmed by research conducted by Harvard psychologist Richard Weissbound. In *The Parents We Mean to Be,* he advocates developing a strong sense of self in children by weaving in values such as responsibility, "to make caring for others as reflexive as breathing."[30]

Weissbound concludes from his research that too much emphasis on our children's happiness and too little on their responsibility for others is "likely to make children not only less moral but, ironically, less happy."[31]

Which brings us back to the Milton Mayeroff philosophy that feeling "in-place" results from "living a life significantly grounded in caring." Stated another way, Frederick Buechner describes vocation as "the place where your deep gladness meets the world's deep need."[32]

Over and over again, Maxine has heard the voice that guided her to this place, the same quality that, after twenty-one years, led me back to her.

What will it be like when the waiting is over? What will happen when we meet our Creator face-to-face? What will it be like to hear God's voice, as we stand before the One who breathed life into us?

Maxine's husband spent his last four days in a hospice bed set up in their living room, where it was affirmed that the waiting is met with glory.

"He reached for my hand, and he mouthed the words 'I love you,'" she recalls. "Then he closed his eyes and all of a sudden he opened them real wide, looked up and smiled, and I said, 'He sees Jesus,' and sure enough, as soon as Judy read the 23rd Psalm, he closed his eyes and died."

Maxine has prepared herself for her own such moment. It only takes a short time in her presence to recognize the spiritual clues. With a similar sense of eagerness, she has tended to the logistics, as well. She has met with the funeral director, picked out her casket, and cashed in her Prudential policy to cover the expenses. She has specified the pastor to preach at her funeral service and the amount that Gary should pay him. She wants three close friends to give eulogies, and joked recently with one of them, "Now, Jane, don't you dare go before I do!" She would like the pastor's son, the church's youth director, to sing "It is Well With My Soul."

"And then I have a dress that I want to be buried in, and I have a plastic bag over it," Maxine explains. "It's pink. Then on the back of the hanger, I have a little grocery bag—one of those plastic bags—and I have a bra, a pair of panties, and a pair of white socks in that. Then I have a box with a brand new wig in it, and I styled it and then I put it back in the box, and I have it marked 'funeral wig.' It's in my bedroom."

This woman is not afraid to die. She could go today, she says, and be happy, except for her children's sake. It would be hard on them, she realizes.

"So I said, 'Lord, let me live till . . .' Actually, I want to live until the Rapture. It could take place any day, according to the Bible. . . ."

Maxine waits "as a bride adorns herself with her jewels."[33] She waits with hope. Waiting, when viewed from her perspective, is not a bad thing. It can be filled with joyous expectancy, the preparation a glorious part of the process.

Which of her personality traits, I ask, would Maxine like family and friends to remember about her?

"Well," she says, "I always like to encourage people. Every day I pray, 'Lord, who can I encourage today?'"

I look at my friend sitting across the sofa, knowing this very quality to be true about her. God knows how hard it is for me to wait, how eager for answers, to move along efficiently, effectively. If Maxine is the hopeful bride, then I am the impatient bridesmaid, tapping her watch, stomping her foot, anxious for the Giver of gifts to step on it. I tell

Maxine about the struggle I've been experiencing with my work, the difficulty in finding direction. She understands and, at the same time, believes that I will get there.

When it is time for me to leave, we stand in the kitchen, light streaming through the side door's window. I ask Maxine to send up a prayer for me—for guidance and for clarity.

"I will," she promises. "And I'll keep praying, too. Let's say a prayer right now." And there between the range and the kitchen table, my friend takes my hands. We close our eyes. She gives thanks for the time we spent together and asks God to watch over me.

"Lord, please direct Jan in what she's supposed to do," she says, "because she's willing to do your will. Lead her and let her know exactly what it is . . ."

Afterward, her soul-blue eyes look directly at me, making my heart feel tended to.

"I know the Lord will lead you and help you," she assures me. "He will."

## My Mother's Bracciola

Round steak, sliced thin
One or two eggs
Parmesan cheese
Fresh garlic, chopped
Fresh parsley, chopped
Salt
Black pepper

There are no specific measurements on this recipe my mother left behind, leaving the rest of us to wing it, as she did. Set yourself free in the kitchen with this one; it's worth the effort!

Beat egg with black pepper, salt, parsley, Parmesan cheese, and garlic. Spread on meat. Roll up and tie with string. Brown in oil. Cook in tomato sauce—long and slow to flavor the sauce. Serve with pasta.

[Hint: You may want to snip off the string before devouring the delectables.]

Chapter Three

# the discernment committee

*I've seen and met angels*
*wearing the disguise of ordinary people*
*living ordinary lives.*

—Tracy Chapman

Ice crystallizes around the windowpanes, darkness has curled in, yet it is bright and warm near the space heater in Mildred's sitting room. Our stomachs are filled with homemade soup and pinwheel sandwiches from Costco. Francie, a longtime member of our prayer group who has moved away and now occasionally returns, sits cross-legged on the floor, pushing her straight brown hair behind her ear, as she reads aloud from her journal. The remaining five of us have been supporting our friend in her effort to determine whether or not to pursue seminary study.

Formally, a group of seekers such as this is known as a discernment committee; its role is to help discern God's will, often for those contemplating entering ministry or for a church seeking a new leader. Now Francie pauses and looks up from the journal, overwhelmed by gratitude.

"Wouldn't it be lovely," she says, "if anyone contemplating a significant life change—not only those giving thought to the ministry—had the support of a discernment committee, people to pray and open channels for listening to a guiding voice?"

The idea strikes me as brilliant: groups of people coming together to pray for discernment regarding which way to go as we meander through life. A change of career. Relocation. The choice of colleges. A commitment to a person, place, job, trip, project, lifestyle, ministry, or cause.

But wait. Isn't this the kind of support already granted? The committee may not gather for Tuesday night meetings; its members may not even recognize their involvement, but there they are at crucial points, illuminating the path. After hugging my prayer group friends good-bye, the thought returns to me. Feathery snow brushes easily from my windshield, and an encourager of my own revisits me as the traffic crawls west on Route 30 toward home.

I think back to a time when I first dabbled in writing poetry. It was not long after I'd mastered cursive writing and the basics of spelling in elementary school. Some of the earliest poems I wrote were gifts to my dad, a tenacious first-generation Italian-American who had a big heart. I can still see his Chevy Impala swinging into our driveway at Christmas, Easter, and Thanksgiving, packed with kids from St. Christopher's Orphanage coming to share the holidays with us.

These early endeavors at writing were Christmas gifts for Dad, sometimes two or three pages long, a dozen or more stanzas. They were attempts at humor, sometimes accompanied by a gift like a cord to hold Dad's reading glasses around his neck, since they never seemed to be where he was when he needed them.

One poem I wrote addressed the many expenses generated, in part, by my needs the preceding year: orthodontics, new glasses, the family vacation we had taken to Florida. The poem purported to rejuvenate his cash flow by providing a "money seed," which was actually some kind of nut in a shell that I'd dug out of the Thanksgiving nut bowl. According to the poem, all Dad had to do was plant the seed, and a tree would spring up with dollar bills dangling from its branches.

On Christmas morning, I could hardly wait for him to open my gift. On went his glasses, and as he read my poem aloud, he would laugh, or a tear would come to his eye.

At the time, I had no clue that this sequence of events was nurturing a passion within me for writing. In fact, years went by without a thought of these early attempts as I embarked upon a career involving various forms of the craft.

After Dad died, a large cardboard box of his, tied with brown string, made its way to the basement of my home. When it first arrived, I opened it and discovered hundreds of cards given to him through the years by his daughters and grandchildren. It took me off guard to learn that he, a staunch businessman, had saved all these sentiments—from Hallmark to handmade. But then again, it made sense: Family meant everything to him. Overwhelmed by grief, I closed the box and stored it.

A year or so later, I came upon it again and decided to reopen it. There, among the keepsakes, were the poems I'd written decades before, each in my youthful handwriting:

the one about the eyeglasses cord, the one about the money seed, even the money seed itself, displayed on a yellowing piece of cotton in a small white box.

The words on one of the cards were penned in turquoise ink, their rhymes adolescent. Its construction paper was worn, red fading to pink, brittle, close to crumbling. Gingerly, I flipped it over. On the back of the card, in my father's handwriting, was this note: "Christmas 1962 from my Jan. My best Christmas gift. Dad."

Like the box piled with cards, my heart grew full. His scribbling, half a century old now, was new to me. Most likely, I was the first to read it. Suddenly the loss of this man and his relentless encouragement cut so deeply, it was as though he'd just died when, in fact, it had been years since the leukemia robbed us of him. Tears dampened the paper, darkening the fading—my Jan, my best Christmas gift—and then it dawned on me: This is why I am a writer. The discovery, this sudden understanding that my father had nurtured the spark in me, felt God-breathed.

Now back from the prayer group meeting, I pull into the garage. Droplets of melted snow glisten, arched beyond the reach of windshield wipers. The ignition clicks off, the engine is stilled, and it occurs to me that Dad may have been the earliest member of my discernment committee, helping me hear a beckoning voice.

The snow has been heavier than usual this year, knee-high on some occasions. Outside the kitchen window, in his bulky green coat, Randy cranks up the snow blower. Soon he'll pop in for his briefcase before making the trek to his graphic design studio, several blocks from home. The serenity of our empty nest—no need to check the television for school closings, no discussion about packing or buying—is familiar now. But with the luxury of solitude comes a certain pressure, too, the expectation that the voice I am seeking will readily be heard. The process, though, even in seclusion, is not like television on demand. We don't control it. It requires staying tuned in, always.

As I pull glasses from the dishwasher, the seed planted by Francie continues to sprout in my mind. Memories blossom, and in this way, a kind of retroactive listening emerges, revealing what seems to have been a perfectly synchronized chorus of angels affirming the natural instincts that led to my choice of vocation. The simple recollection of a second-grade provocation conjures the notion of divine instigation. For who understands my trigger points better than my Creator?

Clean silverware clinks into place in the kitchen drawer, and I think back to recess one day, when a classmate named Karen Cook and I were swinging on the wrought-iron railing leading up the side steps of Aspinwall Elementary School. Karen's hair was pin-straight, tidy, held back by a thin plaid headband. Mine was frizzy and erratic, the kind that, when viewed in school photos, compelled Mother to ask, "Didn't anyone have a comb?"

"I brang a banana flip in my lunch today," I announced.

Karen stopped swinging.

"Brang is not a word," she said.

"Ya-huh."

"Nuh-uh."

"Yes, it is," I insisted. "My mother says it all the time."

Karen locked her hands on her hips.

"Well. It's not a word."

Questioning Mother's word choice had never occurred to me, but the possibility that something was askew must have made me curious. Before long, I started paying closer attention in English, vocabulary, and spelling classes. I was infatuated with grammar. I longed to diagram sentences the way others couldn't wait to get outside to play dodgeball. Later, in college, I would elect to take enough English courses to qualify for both a major and a minor in the subject.

What became of Karen Cook, whether she went on to become a distinguished linguist, a World Book Encyclopedia editor, or a prosecuting attorney, I cannot say. Perhaps our brief confrontation on the second-grade playground triggered a passion in her, as well. Either way, the possibility that intrigues me now is that a seven-year-old smarty-pants, not to mention a mother whose grammar was less than flawless, were also, in some upside-down way, members of my discernment committee. Both were messengers unaware of the impact they delivered.

Randy kicking snow off his boots startles me back into the present. He peeks into the kitchen from the laundry room.

"Phew, it's cold out there." His cheeks are red, his glasses fogged. "Newspaper says it's supposed to dip into the teens."

I've been listening to the music of memory, not prone to switching to the weather channel. My lost-in-reverie expression must reveal that an idea is brewing, for Randy nods.

"Just hand me my briefcase, will you?" he asks. "And I'll be out of here."

Like Paul, who, in his letters to Timothy, showed understanding of Timothy's struggles in ministry, my husband knows the creative process.

"Fight the good fight," Paul wrote to his friend who was enduring some of the same problems he himself had experienced, "holding onto faith and a good conscience."

Randy is aware of my endeavor to sharpen my listening and that the finest brand of support he can offer is giving me space when I need it. The door clicks behind him, and I retrieve a small tablet from the kitchen junk drawer. With an English muffin warming in the toaster oven, I sit at the island and start jotting down names of those who, unknowingly, composed my discernment committee, a list to which I will later return at my computer: Dad, Karen Cook, Mother, Mrs. Widgery . . .

Mrs. Widgery was my twelfth-grade English teacher, a lanky, dark-haired woman with a tender voice. Also a novelist, she had penned a best seller, *The Adversary*, though at the time, I was unfamiliar with the magnitude of this status, nor did it occur to my sixteen-year-old self how fortunate I was to be under her tutelage.

One afternoon, Mrs. Widgery appeared at the door of the school library. In front of the window was a row of vinyl-clad chairs, and I sat studying in one of them. My teacher was holding a typewritten paper as she approached me and, as we were taught at our school, I stood in her presence.

"I've been looking all over for you," she said.

The paper she held was a short story I'd turned in for a writing assignment. Mrs. Widgery pointed to the page, and in a whisper that was loud enough for others to hear, she praised an image in it. To this day, I remember: It was a description of a little girl standing abandoned on a beach, drenched with rain, and pulling her soaked T-shirt away from her stomach.

I don't remember what it was about the image that appealed to her—the level of detail, I think—but here was a woman who knew how to reach the writer in me. The affirmation I felt, as a high school senior, from my teacher's effort to seek me out must have been akin to the moment that she herself had received word of her book's extraordinary recognition.

A glint of sunlight sparkles through the kitchen window as I sink my teeth into the English muffin and add more names to my list: a colleague named Sue, my dear friend Howard. Each day God's voice arrives in unique ways—like Francie's offhand remark and books that I encounter. The idea of a personal support network—this group that seems born of divine inspiration—is a recurring theme, as though God is in conversation with me, affirming my discoveries.

In *God's Voice Within*, author and spiritual director Mark E. Thibodeaux writes, "As I make my way through the spiritual life, it is absolutely crucial that I have a strong support network following close behind me, cheering me on, booing the false spirit, whispering tips in my ear, and passing me Gatorade."[34]

In *The Council of Dads,* cancer-stricken author Bruce Feiler describes how, in an effort to leave a legacy of voices for his young twin daughters, he reached out to six men who had helped shape him. Based on their unique qualities, he invited them to participate in his daughters' upbringing, knowing the distinct message each would convey: how to travel, how to live, how to dream, etc.

"Overnight they became a meaningful presence in the girls' lives," he writes, "a new figure that was different from family, deeper than a friend."

Now cancer free, Feiler notes that the Council still plays an important role. "It's the most uplifting community we've ever created; it helps us through adversity; and it reminds us every day to celebrate the friendships we are blessed to have."[35]

The tavern at the General Sutter Inn is quiet this evening, just one couple sitting at the bar. A flickering candle lights the corner table near the window, where my friend Sue and I are having dinner. It's been at least two years since we last got together, but as always, our conversation is unencumbered by the lapses, easily picking up where we left off. Our friendship has spanned four decades now.

In our early twenties, Sue and I worked side by side in the front office of an advertising agency. I'd taken a clerical position there in the hope of someday landing a copywriting job. I had little to show in the way of samples, other than pieces I'd written in college: essays, poetry, a three-act play. But Sue, who worked there as a bookkeeper and in whom I'd confided, encouraged me to collect my best work and slip it onto our boss's desk.

"Maybe he'll see a spark," she urged. "What could it hurt?"

We were two young women at the bottom of the totem pole, one trying to boost up the other. Her encouragement led to a major milestone for me: the launch of my writing career. Eventually, we each moved on to start businesses of our own and are now both engaged in new endeavors. As usual, the talking is nonstop, as we catch up on families, her new job, my writing, her trip to St. John.

Since I've been thinking about personal discernment committees as vehicles to amplify God's voice, my friend's role in encouraging me back when we were twentysome-things has been on my mind, and I want her to know how much that gesture meant to me. We glance at the dessert menu. She orders coffee; I order tea.

"There's something I want to thank you for," I say. "It happened back when we were at Kelly, and I wanted so badly to be a copywriter. I don't know if you remember, but you egged me on . . ."

"I know. You already thanked me."

"I did?"

"Yes, years ago you wrote me a letter acknowledging that very thing."

"Really? I don't remember."

We laugh, because just minutes ago we were agreeing that sometimes it feels as though we are completely losing our memories.

"I still have the letter," she adds. And then she surprises

me even more. "I actually had it framed."

She continues talking about the frame, the matting, the way she wanted the letter centered, but the voice that rises above hers is that of the Holy Spirit, reminding me of who put this woman on my path.

During the weeks following my dinner with Sue, I continue thinking about others who seem to have comprised a divinely commissioned tag team, running by my side. One morning, a message pops up in my email inbox from a long-time mentor, a cherished friend whose name was prominent on my list. Howard lives near Philadelphia, about sixty miles away from my Lancaster County home, and we don't see each other often; we keep in touch mainly by email. Today's message is written in typical Howard style:

> i was in two minds whether to send this to you or not
>
> i know you being you might be inclined to come
>
> but me being me would say it's not at all necessary
>
> still, if you heard about it and had not been invited
>
> you might have been hurt/upset
>
> and i would never want that
>
> Jan, i feel that even if we never sent another email never visited
>
> what we have forged goes so deep and would be so
>
> lasting it needs nothing more
>
> (howard, will you PLEASE GET ON WITH IT
>
> I HAVE ONLY ANOTHER HOUR BEFORE I HAVE TO LEAVE!)

ok

they are having a retirement luncheon for me at Temple University
Rhoads Room of the Diamond Club, Mitten Hall, Temple Campus,
noon, April 27 and if you can't make it in person, know that you
still will be there: because you are one of the most important
people in my life EVER

The Rhoads Room in Temple University's Mitten Hall is
buzzing with people whose lives have been touched by Howard: students representing each of the four decades that
he's taught writing and broadcast advertising in tandem with
his advertising career, colleagues, women from his cancer
survivors' writing workshops, family.

The twenty-three-year-old sitting next to me, a bright
woman named Jewel, tells me that she met Howard at the
frozen yogurt parlor where she works. He, a customer who
learned of her interest in writing, proposed a challenge in
which he'd give her a prompt, she'd write about it, and he'd
buy her any book that she wanted. The bargain was struck,
the writing continued, and a young woman received encouragement that was so meaningful to her that here she is at his
retirement luncheon. The story has Howard's name written
all over it; a profound influence arises from his caring. I know.
I have been blessed to be a recipient of it, too. Meeting Jewel
takes me back to my early encounters with him decades ago.

At age twenty-nine, the divorced mother of a five-year-
old, I was about to leave the security of my job at a Fortune

500 company to embark on a venture of my own. I'd given notice, but my impending departure hadn't been formally announced, so I was stunned one morning when, after a meeting, Howard confronted me about it. The Philadelphia firm in which he was a partner serviced the retail advertising needs of our department, and my colleagues and I typically met with Howard every Tuesday. Those meetings and the occasional lunches I shared with him had shown him to be one of the most human of human beings—to borrow a phrase that he himself uses sparingly to describe others—and so I listened.

The others had left the conference room, and Howard and I remained seated across the table from one another. His extensive experience—at least a dozen more years than I had—gave him firsthand knowledge of the risks of entering a "dog-eat-dog business" with no paycheck or benefits. "Especially," he noted, "for someone with a soft heart." He felt compelled to point out the pitfalls. He suggested a more conservative approach to starting my ad agency by working at it nights and weekends, while maintaining my corporate income and perks, until I was sure it was taking off. But I'd already been freelancing on weekends and nights after my daughter was asleep; the increased workload was taking a toll. One of the jobs had to go, and I'd chosen to turn the freelance endeavor, with its entrepreneurial appeal, into a full-time business. I shared this information with him.

"But what if you starve?" Howard challenged from across the conference table.

"That won't happen," I said, my determination solidifying.

"It won't?"

"I can be thrifty when I have to."

"How?" he prodded. "Give me one example of how you can be thrifty."

I was grateful for his caring—it is one of his endearing qualities—but I was ready to wrap this up. He'd made his point and, to tell the truth, it was hard thinking of an example of my thriftiness when there were so few of them.

"Did you ever notice in the grocery store that yellow napkins cost more than white napkins?" I posed. Honest to God, this is what popped into my mind. "I prefer yellow napkins, but to save a few cents, I would be willing to make the switch."

Later that day, after lunch, I returned to my office. I hung my sweater behind my door, and when I turned around, there on my chair was a jumbo-sized package of five hundred yellow napkins. On that day, this straightforward, big-hearted man became one of the staunchest and most trusted members of my discernment committee—a mentor, a friend—who cares enough to question, yet always affirms the person I was meant to be.

Those we choose as mentors, according to Thibodeaux, should not be afraid to confront us when they think we are wrong. When someone challenges our thinking, it can enrich the discernment process by compelling us to consider perspectives that may otherwise have not occurred. It can also test our determination, helping us to distinguish passion from passing whim.

Now, as the room grows quiet, I think about the young

woman next to me and how fortunate she is, especially at her age, to have found a mentor in Howard. A couple of his colleagues rise to speak at the podium, one claiming that there is no finer man than Howard, another joking that, in the eyes of the students, "He makes the rest of us look bad." A dean stands with a hefty pile of evaluation forms and reads heartfelt student comments ranking my friend's classes among the department's most popular.

Finally at the podium himself, Howard offers a mosaic of experiences from his teaching years. One recalls an assignment he gave students to demonstrate sentence variety in writing about their best friend, who often turned out to be a parent. After they shared their essays in class, Howard requested that the students read their piece to the one about whom it was written, give that person a copy, and then share the recipient's reaction with the class. Students would hem and haw.

"Do you want to pass this course?" Howard would ask.

They looked at him wide-eyed and stammered, "Yes, I do want to pass the course," hoping their professor would forget about this part of the assignment. But he never did.

"Roger, what did your mother say when you read your piece to her?"

"She didn't say anything. She just cried."

His story reminds me of a time many years ago, when, fearing Dad's death, I shared with Howard over lunch one day the profound ways my father had influenced me. Howard urged me to share these memories with my father. Like the students, I flinched.

"I cannot imagine my daughter feeling this way about me and telling a complete stranger instead of telling me," he insisted. "I would want to know."

The following Christmas, I wrote my sentiments in a letter, read it privately to my father, and then gave it to him. We hugged that day and, clearing his throat, Dad said that a parent could not receive a finer gift. Years later, after he died, I would empty the contents of his desk drawers and find photocopies of the letter—and then, in his dresser drawers, more photocopies of the same letter.

As Howard speaks of the young men and women he's had the privilege of teaching, he shares having "viewed them not just as students in a writing workshop or a media advertising class but also as young people at a pivotal point in their lives." And so he felt compelled to share with them the practical (the value of 401ks), the philosophical ("success is never final; failure is never fatal"), and the fact that perception is reality. He asked them to think about a question that a corporate CEO asked of those she interviewed: "What are you doing when you feel most beautiful? What are you doing when you are shining, when you're in the zone, when you're on fire? What are you doing when you feel this way?"

Listening to Howard, it occurs to me that I, too, have had the privilege of being his student. Over the seventeen years that my ad agency grew, he was there for me. He was someone I could call for advice or when I needed a kindred spirit or the clarity of thinking at which he excels. It was a time of many graces: a business partner who, several years in, joined the firm and with whom I felt proud to be associated, dozens of quality-driven employees from whom I learned and with whom I grew, clients who believed in us, accolades won, the satisfaction of a job well done.

It is an old story: The more the business grew, the more my energy turned toward management and away from the creative process that had been integral to its birth. I could write pages about how to delegate and how not to, but that isn't the point. The markers were there: the lure back to writing, not to mention a second young daughter who, I knew after having raised one seventeen years older, would be all grown up in a heartbeat. I was remarried now and blessed to have built a marketable business; the choice to move on was within my grasp, and the timing seemed right.

"But you can't leave!" Howard challenged. "You *are* the agency."

I looked at my trusted friend and mentor, now sitting across another conference table from me. I did not remind him that he was the one who had convinced me to attend the writer's conference that reignited my passion for writing, advice that I did take and for which I will always be grateful. But as usual, the discussion drove straight to the heart of my intentions, testing my commitment, affirming that I was sure. Whether or not he agreed with my decision was never the issue. The gift comes when we find that our paths have been illuminated by people who have the courage to care, to disagree and challenge, while respecting where the final determination—whether right or wrong—belongs.

"What are you doing when you feel most beautiful?" the professor asks.

I am opening up to the voice of all goodness—a sacred voice that emanates from a half-century-old note scribbled on back of a handmade card, from five hundred yellow napkins, and from words that arise in my heart for me to pass along to others.

## My Mother's Pasta with Cauliflower

3 tablespoons oil
Small onion, chopped
Head of cauliflower, chopped
Salt and pepper

You don't need to heat the oil alone.
Put onion, then cauliflower into oil on stovetop.
Add salt and pepper, to taste.
Brown all together.
Add two cups of water and simmer.
Serve over pasta.

# *subtracting*

*Simplicity means not being complicated,*
*not being double in any way,*
*not deluding oneself or anyone else . . .*
*we cease to want to be rich, successful or popular,*
*and want instead the things that satisfy our*
*deeper instincts.*

—Caryll Houselander

The question "What are you doing when you feel most beautiful?" raises an opposite challenge, as well: "What are you doing when you feel ugliest?" Today my work pushes me away. I cannot decipher what it wants of me. I long to pull it close, to tenderly embrace it. But like a child in a tantrum, it won't let me near. The connection has been severed. I try to coax disparate pieces together, but the harder I push, the messier it becomes. This overbearing effort is what I am doing when I feel ugliest.

Hours pass. Crumpled paper dots the floor. I sharpen pencils as though pointier points will produce proficiency. It seems that time has slithered away, leaving me nowhere, though some might argue that failure is simply part of the process. I grab a jacket, close the door behind me, and head for the wooded path off Oak Street. At first, the writing follows, sulking and accusing me of abandonment. If I am not at peace with my own voice, how can I hear that of God? Or is it the other way around?

The early peek of spring, the promising buds, pulls hikers and bikers outdoors. An old stone farmhouse sits off to the left of the trail, a gurgling stream nearby. A clan of ladybugs gathers to sunbathe. It must have been the grace of God that led us to this small town with the down-to-earth charm of a Norman Rockwell painting—the subtle aroma from the Wilbur Chocolate factory, the shops along Main Street. The world in which I live wasn't always this uncomplicated.

There was a time, long before we moved here, when Randy and I were agreeing to plunk down the initiation fees to join a country club, to add a carriage house behind our custom-built home, to sail the Caribbean in the presidential suite of a luxury cruise liner. Making these decisions was as simple as pulling the checkbook from a drawer. Then I sold my advertising agency for the freedom to stay at home, where I could greet my kindergartner at the bus stop each day, where I would sit at my dying father's bedside, where I would write my first book.

Before long, we were facing an uncharacteristic financial slump, and we weren't sure how long we could tolerate the throes of a negative cash flow. And there was something else. A verse. While I was thumbing through the pages of the Bible, a passage jumped out at me, started waving a flag with my name on it. So compelling were the words that I copied them onto a yellow Post-It, stuck it to my dashboard, and prayed it every time I got in the car. "Turn my eyes away from worthless things; preserve my life according to your word."[36]

The day we pulled up to a dollhouse-sized Tudor, which was to become our new home, I took in its mismatched brick, the lopsided antenna on the slate roof, the rusted air conditioner propped in a window, and wondered if God was answering my prayer.

"God is not found in the soul by adding anything," wrote fourteenth-century theologian Meister Eckhart, "but by subtracting."

The longer I live, the more fully I grasp that clearing away clutter is vital for hearing the Spirit's voice. Experience has taught me that simplification doesn't happen overnight or even in a month. After so many years of adding, of complicating and indulging, subtracting takes commitment. It means peeling back one leaf at a time, like those of Mother's stuffed artichokes, each one filled with delicious discovery, but none quite so much as the prize at the heart.

My walk refreshes me—the crispness in the air, the picturesque horses strong and well-groomed at Linden Hall's stables. The cardinals have returned to nest in our hedges. Back in my study, I remember the first time Randy and I stood in the doorway of this room. It had aged floral wallpaper, a radiator crusty with peeling paint, old metal blinds.

"What would we use this for?" he asked.

"I'll take it," I volunteered, imagining freshly painted walls, a refinished floor, and built-in bookshelves. "It could be my study."

"But it would be depressing,"

"No, it wouldn't," I objected. "There are five windows in here!"

An architect friend affirmed the house's "good bones," and the viability of remodeling on our budget. Still, the change would be significant, and we weren't sure. So when the real estate agent called to inform us that another offer was being presented that evening, our hearts started pounding.

"I just want to do whatever God wants," I admitted to my husband. "I wish God would make it clear."

Within fifteen minutes, the kind voice of a friend, a trusted financial advisor, came through the telephone.

"You're making the right decision," he said.

Now, the new casing around the living room fireplace is painted white and flanked by two miniature six-paned windows. These were the windows that, when I first stood taking in their craftsmanship, made me realize, *I think I can live here.*

Though we can't see the manicured fairway, as we could from our former house, it is a ten-minute stroll to Dosie Dough for bagels and tea. A short distance beyond that is a park with a stream, ducks, and little stone bridges. There is no in-home theater like the one we left behind, no three-car garage, no spare bedroom, no carriage house, no neighborhood tennis court, no community security gates that require a pass card to enter.

But outside my study windows stands a towering maple that must have been planted eight decades ago. There is a trail of paver stones amid the hydrangeas, and neighbors fluent in the city's history.

Subtracting, I've learned, is a repeat process. It requires

vigilance. At first, our yearnings for more may seem to be conquered, but then there they are again.

"God is not a God of disorder but of peace,"[37] notes one of the verses that calls my name. Peace, as in releasing that which causes clutter. As in letting go. As in opening up to hear a sacred voice.

Howard once suggested that if people had slogans, as corporations do, mine would be one word: strive. This is true. I am in a constant state of striving, which stirs up a racket and undermines calm. Striving to exercise, striving to check off to-do lists, striving to lighten up on striving.

In the process of downsizing to a smaller home, cleaning out the basement of our old house took days. The number of throw pillows alone that I had accumulated and stored would cause eyebrows to raise. There was much paring back to do, and I was not the first to discover the liberating feeling that blooms from doing so.

But then came the arrival at our new home, the unpacking, the settling in. To my surprise, box after box of throw pillows remained in my possession, enough of them, in fact, to fill an unfinished closet under the eaves of our remodeled house. Other than a few suitcases, that entire closet now houses them—shelves of pillows. My nickname for this space—if you wouldn't mind keeping a secret—is the "pillow garage."

Throw pillows, in moderation, spruce up a room. A dash of color here, a cozy print there, but too many of them can make finding a place to sit, well, awkward. Visitors perch on the sofa's edge, trying to be polite.

"Just toss them out of the way," I offer.

Accessories decorating the surfaces of my home are not the only signs of cluttering. There is the calendar bursting with commitments, the cell phone dinging in my purse, the tendency to scatter the word *yes* as freely as pillows across the furniture.

"If clutter is thought of as a kind of interfering noise, like static," writes philosopher Milton Mayer, "there is a certain quieting that goes with simplification."[38]

Clutter can distract from that which is simple and true. If I am to hear the Spirit's promptings and even my own voice, I need to steer clear of noise. This lesson has been offered to me time and again; God is incredibly patient.

A couple of years after we downsized to a home nearly half the size of our previous one, we acquired a small getaway in the mountains of Western Pennsylvania. Our purchase of the Treehouse, as we affectionately call it, was made possible through the generosity of my late parents (which in no way implicates them). In no time, the complications were back, throw pillows and all. A passion for decorating returned with such gumption that I nearly traded a fulfilling vocation for it. A friend I hadn't seen in decades reentered my life on what I now see as a sacred and strategic timetable. A long-ago high school pal, Marilyn was as practical as ever.

"Do you have a bucket?" she asked.

Through the Treehouse windows, the afternoon sun slithered over the Laurel Highlands as we talked about hiking with our golden retrievers now that our families owned neighboring vacation homes here.

"Yes, I have a bucket. Why?"

"You're going to need it to wash the mud off Sammi's feet."

"But it's a new bucket," I objected.

"Uh-huh." Marilyn looked expectant, as though I might make a point.

"And it's white," I added.

My friend squinted. She did not say, "So what?" but her brain was thinking it so loudly that I could not help but overhear.

Had something gone awry in the free-spirited sixteen-year-old with whom Marilyn had once spent Friday nights cruising the suburbs of Pittsburgh? I can still see the two of us frequenting Eat'n Park, flinging short-lived diets to the wind in favor of Big Boys and fries, then heading to Baskin-Robbins for God-knows-how-many flavors stacked heaping high on cones.

How did it get to the point that Marilyn could name the species of every bird that came to roost on her feeder, while my mind's Rolodex zeroed in on freshening up the bird-house with a new Benjamin Moore paint color? I will not tell you how much I once spent for a throw pillow cut of antique cloth, because you would consider me out of my mind or think of a nobler expenditure, all of which would be true and does, in fact, point to an issue of mine.

Scripture goes right for the jugular on the subject: "For where your treasure is, there your heart will be also."[39]

*The Message* translation of the Bible makes the warning even more ominous: "Don't hoard treasure down here. . . . stockpile treasure in heaven, where it's safe from moth and rust and burglars. It's obvious, isn't it? The place where your treasure is, is the place you will most want to be, and end up being."[40]

In a pillow garage? With decorative cushions?

This love affair with all things beautiful did not start and stop with buckets and throw pillows. My former career afforded me the luxury to indulge myself. If only I could say I resisted, but there were French-inspired wall clocks, nine ottomans, Turkish rugs, and mahogany sideboards—of which I amassed three.

The subject is not popular with my husband, as laid back as he may be. He might recall a word game we once played on a road trip with our younger daughter. In the car's back seat, Katherine read the game card prompts.

"A man's name that begins with an 'R'!"

"Ralph!" I shouted without hesitation.

Randy rolled his eyes. "My own wife thinks of the name of a furniture designer before she thinks of mine."

I believed that my priorities proved properly ordered when, after seventeen years, I sold my business for the chance to stay at home with my young daughter and follow my passion for writing. And again, when we downsized. For years, my widowed mother entertained my penchant for design, having arrived from Florida without a stick of furniture, and then moving five times along the continuing care continuum. With no little sarcasm, she dubbed me her "interior decorator." Décor meant little to her, but upon each move, she shrugged and accepted my furniture arrangements (over which I'd labored on floor-plan grids), the paint colors I chose, the accessories. It was a feast in home fashions, as well as a way of giving something of myself to her. She pooh-poohed the fuss, but I wish she could have felt deserving.

Now with Mother gone, the Treehouse provided a clean slate for indulging my impulse and buoying my spirits. Perhaps this passion for creating comfort addressed my need to fix that which seemed irreparable and now, after her death, even more so. The impetus was so strong that I would have rather served broth for dinner than walk past a sale on table lamps. I revisited room plans, fiddling with templates, a corner cupboard here, an end table over there. My husband, at this point bearing the brunt of our breadwinning, began to drop hints.

"You should be writing," he said. "The Treehouse is beautiful just as it is."

And he was right. The clutter of outside noise at full volume—the disruptions, the busyness—makes my writing feel small, unimportant. In the whispers, nuggets wait to be heard. Still, I turned down catalogue page corners and dialed 800 numbers. It was hard not to want the linen pillow with the faux horn button.

And then, what looked like a lifeline appeared. It was the possibility of assisting a talented interior designer. It sounded like a productive way to channel my impulses and hone my skills at the same time. The idea was tantalizing: a steady paycheck, the fabrics, the colors, the patterns, the textures, the buying, the arranging, the accessorizing.

The trade-off, of course, was not insignificant. It would mean putting the writing on hold, missing my teenager's tennis matches, the after-school ice cream at Greco's. These were the very things for which, less than a decade earlier, I'd traded in a lucrative career.

I needed to pray about this.

Luke tells a story in the Bible that makes people like me cringe. It is about a rich, young ruler who has it all—power, possessions, prestige, money—and asks Jesus how he can gain eternal life. Jesus starts reciting the Ten Commandments, and the rich man interrupts, saying that he knows all those; he's been keeping them since he was a kid.

So Jesus gives it to him straight: Sell all your stuff, give the proceeds to the poor, and follow me. This is too much for the self-sufficient guy to wrap his brain around, so he pushes the "no deal" button and walks away.

Jesus then says that "it is easier for a camel to go through the eye of a needle than for someone who is rich to enter the kingdom of God."[41]

The rich person parable isn't about wealth or fame, but about how we find ultimate fulfillment. It's about the choices we make for tending to our souls: prestige or power, food or booze, fame or furnishings—or a Spirit that endures. Sometimes we hold on so tightly to the throw pillows, or whatever else muffles the pain, that the still, small voice inside—the sacred, the spiritual—gets buried, too.

Jesus said that the greatest commandment is to "Love the Lord your God with all your heart and with all your soul and with all your mind."[42] The second greatest, he asserted, is to "Love your neighbor as yourself."[43] The decision before me wasn't whether one vocation or the other afforded the ability to live out God's will. Either could open those doors. But which path was better for *me*? I prayed for clarification while, truthfully, campaigning for indulgence.

Then one day, a Bible sat open on my lap. Preparing for a study group, I was just digging in. And this was the verse hurled at me: "Her foes have become her masters; her enemies are at ease. The Lord has brought her grief because of her many sins."[44]

A bit unnerved, I flipped to another page. "If you will not listen to me and carry out all these commands, and if you reject my decrees and abhor my laws and fail to carry out all my commands and so violate my covenant, then I will do this to you . . . "

The consequences are too terrifying even to enumerate, but if you insist on knowing, you can check out Leviticus 26:14–17, the verses on which my defiant hands landed. It did not take a spiritual guru to grasp that God is not big on sending an alcoholic to work at the wine and spirits store. My propensity to elevate Portuguese pottery and Jacquard table linens to the status of idols is no different from a wino gulping straight from the bottle.

Enter Marilyn and the white bucket. It is a holy experience to reconnect with the friend upon whose bed you once sat while she iced your earlobe, holding a potato behind it, as another friend pierced the lobe with a sterilized needle. It gets you thinking about who you've become relative to who you wanted to be. It triggers memories, like the one of a teenager who would have traded her whole pierced-earring collection to do exactly what I am doing right now at 12:55

in the afternoon, still in my bathrobe, listening for words that, hopefully, will matter to others someday. Listening and hearing, receiving and giving.

"I mean, I really like decorating," I told Marilyn one snowy day over a cup of tea. My decision was made, but still, I felt compelled to talk about it. "It's fun to move things around and then stand at the doorway, feeling a sense of harmony. But I don't know if it would be a good place to permanently position myself, or even if it would be as fulfilling a career for me as it is just as a hobby."

"Yeah," she agreed. "It's not like you'd be doing it for Habitat for Humanity or anything." I looked at my friend, appreciative of the heart she had nurtured all these years. And then she added this: "I guess it depends what you want to be doing for the rest of your life."

Amen and amen.

Now here I am, years later, wrestling with work that's been a gift to me. Instead of listening calmly, I worry that I'm finished, no longer hearing thoughts worth exploring. What if I'm discovered as an impostor? Any good that's come from my efforts has purely been accomplished through the Holy Spirit; the goof-ups are mine alone, a reflection of my propensity to grab reins that haven't been offered. Perhaps in place of writing, I should seek a shift at Rosey's Lunch Wagon.

My mother taught me to worry. When I was little, she warned that if I spilled crumbs, we would have ants everywhere. If I didn't jiggle the doorknob three times to make sure it was locked upon leaving home, someone might get into the house and rob us. In the bridal salon where I tried on my wedding dress, she leaned forward when the consultant left the room and, in a loud whisper, cautioned, "Don't tell her where we live; she'll jack up the price on the alterations." Privately (or in concert with my sisters), I rejected my mother's concerns, deeming them ridiculous or annoying. But the fact is that when it comes to imagining the tragedies that might befall me, I was (and still am) my mother's apprentice.

Like an obsession with throw pillows, worry creates static; it impedes the ability to decipher inner voice. Even worse, it's been said that worrying is rooted in pride, one of the Seven Deadly Sins, right up there with envy, gluttony, lust, anger, greed, and sloth. The point is that we can get so distracted by our own limitations that we forget to look away from ourselves and toward the One who has promised never to forsake us.

"Fretting rises from our determination to have our own way," notes Oswald Chambers. "Our Lord never worried and was never anxious, because His purpose was never to accomplish His own plans but to fulfill God's plans. . . . All our fretting and worrying is caused by planning without God."[45]

We worry that our husband will fall off a ladder while trimming the hedges, that our hairdresser's feelings will be hurt because we have decided to try a new stylist named Carmine, that our kids will burn down the house roasting marshmallows in the toaster oven. Some of these things may well happen, and it's hard to trust an abstract promise that our Creator will bring good from every mess in which we find ourselves. Yet the command "Fear not," I've heard, is the one that Jesus repeated most frequently.

"Peace I leave with you; my peace I give you . . . Do not let your hearts be troubled and do not be afraid."[46]

Why, I wonder, did Jesus have to keep repeating himself about this?

"Who of you by worrying can add a single hour to your life?"[47]

Was it because worriers like me are too wrapped up in the minutiae of our own little details to connect to the source of all power?

"I am the Lord your God who takes hold of your right hand and says to you, "Do not fear; I will help you."[48]

Really. Here is our God earnestly reaching out, and some of us are so distracted by worry that it puts Jesus at risk of developing laryngitis.

". . . do not worry about tomorrow for tomorrow will worry about itself. Each day has enough trouble of its own."[49]

Now I learn that three accomplished authors, all of whom write about spiritual matters and whose work I admire, are also plagued by anxiety. My knee-jerk reaction is judgment. As Oswald Chambers poses, "How can we dare to be so absolutely unbelieving when God totally surrounds us?"[50] And then, not once, but three separate times, I am reminded that I am looking in the mirror.

Many writers, I have read, are worriers by nature. Perhaps God gives us words for this very reason: "Here, take tens of thousands of these, and make yourself useful."

"For I know the plans I have for you, . . . plans to prosper you and not to harm you, plans to give you hope and a future."[51]

Somewhere deep in my heart, a voice whispers Mother's name. In the murmur, there is sadness, the reminder of a relationship that fell short of fruition. The false starts, the failed attempts, the disconnection. Is that the buried pain about which my writing begs to speak? Is it I—and not the work—who, in fear, is pushing away? Perhaps I have been, though I do not want to be, the one who, bearing Mother's legacy, cannot hear.

"Be strong and courageous. Do not be afraid; do not be discouraged, for the Lord your God will be with you wherever you go."[52]

## My Mother's Garlic Pizza

2 loaves frozen Italian bread dough

1/4 cup finely chopped fresh garlic

1/3 cup freshly grated Italian cheese

1 tablespoon oregano

2 teaspoons black pepper

1 cup vegetable oil

Thaw bread in refrigerator overnight.

Two hours before baking, roll each bread loaf out with flour and rolling pin. Grease cookie sheet for each pizza. Spread dough evenly over sheet.

Cover with plastic wrap and lay towel on top.

Let dough set for one to two hours. Preheat oven to 350 degrees. Cover dough evenly with garlic, cheese, oregano, black pepper. Last, drizzle with oil, about 1/4 cup per pizza. Takes about 1/2 hour, but you need to switch shelves in oven after 15 minutes and pay close attention to see if pizza is getting too brown.

Chapter Five

# mattering

*Grandfather, Great Spirit,*
*once more behold me on Earth*
*and lean to hear my feeble voice.*
—Black Elk

My weakening knees beg me not to climb onto the arm of the sofa, but it's the most efficient way to reach the upper shelves of my study's bookcase. The novel I'm searching for is nowhere in sight. My hands land on a black hardcover, bound by one-inch spirals. The front features an old photo of my parents and is inscribed with the words "Family Memories." The piece, handmade, was a send-off gift for my parents when they moved from Pittsburgh to Florida and eventually, after they'd died, it found its way to my shelf.

Now it seems that the book is a gift to me, as Mother especially has been on my mind. I pull it down and sit on the sofa, paging through reminiscences offered by those closest to her: daughters, sons-in-law, grandchildren, siblings, nieces and nephews. Page after page, her remembrance is amplified through my family's voices.

*Her bread dough rising on the glider in the basement kitchen; shaking that finger at me to get a point across; her*

*instructions on how to kill my weeds, how to get rid of the
rabbits who were eating my plants, what not to do in order
to protect myself, my family, my garbage disposal; endless card
games of steal-the-pile on the back porch; boiling water being
poured from a pot of perfectly cooked spaghetti noodles; her
sitting near the pool and watching me swim for hours; her
fried dough with cinnamon and sugar; hundreds of meatballs
prepared for the Y-Teens fundraiser; telling me I should have
named Katie, my sixth, "Amen" because it was time to quit having
kids; the aroma of bread baking in the oven. . . .*

I remember that in receiving the gift, Mother nodded a
perfunctory thank you. But later, behind closed doors, she
groused, as she did about gifts in general. She didn't need
any gifts. They just took up space, and she had no room for
them.

Now the book sits closed on my lap. My study is quiet
other than the hum of a distant hedge trimmer. Outside,
the leaves sway against a colorless sky, crisscrossed by wires
above Third Avenue. Perhaps Mother's disdain for gifts
given to please her arose from an unshakeable belief that
she didn't matter. Nothing wrapped in a bow could fill her
emptiness. The thought in my mind rings so true that it must
have been the Spirit who put it there.

Yet from another perspective, her reaction stung.

*I know,* a soothing voice answers. *I know.*

Years ago, on the day that the box filled with freshly
printed books arrived, I tore open the top and pulled one
out. There, in my hands, like a diploma at graduation, was
the manifestation of years of labor and the experiences that

had made it possible. An odd mixture of accomplishment and nostalgia rushed through me. As much as I'd wanted to finish *Riding the Dog,* my first book, I would miss the nourishment and sense of healing that the writing of it had provided.

The cover felt satiny, its sepia-toned photo capturing a slice of family history at a tiny house on Pittsburgh's Winterburn Street. In the picture, my father sits on the front stoop striking a pose, one hand resting against the cement, the other curled at the side of his head. Two of my sisters flank him, Marge leaning against his raised knee, laughing, and Lena kneeling behind, her smile demure. Mother stands, hand on hip, in the darkened doorway behind them. Perhaps my sister Dee shot the photo with a Brownie camera, and Pat—then a toddler—must have been inside napping. I hadn't been born yet.

The pages fluttered as I thumbed through them. To my relief, the chapters were printed in the correct order. This very first copy, I decided, would go to my mother. Now ninety years old, she was living at a nearby retirement community, having moved from Florida several years earlier, after Dad died. She had no clue of the project in which I'd been immersed; the recounting of our final journey with my father would be a complete surprise.

Randy and I arrived at her apartment, which, at the time, was in the facility's independent living wing. Presenting her with the book was a momentous occasion for me, although I knew better than to expect her to strike up a band. But perhaps she'd feel a tinge of pride, the tiniest hint of gladness? She looked at the family photo on the cover.

"Who's that?" she asked, pointing to the blurred figure in the shadowed doorway.

"Well, that's you, Mother," I said.

"I look old," she snapped. And then: "Who wrote this book?"

"I did."

"Uh-huh," she murmured. She laid the book on the kitchen table. "I have to go to bingo now. I save seats there, and I put cards out at my table. Sometimes people win on those cards I put out." Then she swished past Randy and me and headed out the door.

As human beings, we want to matter. There are signs of this everywhere: in our homes and in our garages, at our jobs, and in our jewelry boxes. We want those we love to applaud our efforts. We are filled with hope. Will it serve the needs of thousands? Can it win an award? Will it go viral on YouTube?

And yet, in my heart there's a stirring, a voice that suggests it is so much simpler than that. Like the bingo cards awaiting the arrival of players, God's love is there for us—readily available—if only we will pull up a chair to claim it.

Scripture conveys that *we* are loved not because of who we are, but because of who *God* is. There are no strings attached. Still, the overachievers among us crave a bit more input. We are driven to accomplish the very task that God has in mind for us. I, for one, relentlessly seek "The Divine

Strategic Plan," disregarding the fact that God is so much less anal than I am.

"If we will be what the Scriptures call us to be, then there is a greater likelihood that we will do what it is we are called to perform,"[53] noted one pastor.

"Our Lord calls us to no special work," asserts another. "He calls us to Himself."[54]

Author, teacher, and former pastor Barbara Brown Taylor describes one particular effort of hers to hear God's voice. Upon college graduation, she longed to know God's plan for her vocation, her designated purpose on Earth.

"One night," she writes, "when my whole heart was open to hearing from God what I was supposed to do with my life, God said, 'Anything that pleases you.'

"'What?' I said, resorting to words. . . . 'What kind of an answer is that?'

"'Do anything that pleases you,' the voice in my head said again, 'and belong to me.'

"Whatever I decided to do for a living, it was not what I did but how I did it that mattered. God had suggested an overall purpose, but was not going to supply the particulars for me. If I wanted a life of meaning, then I was going to have to apply the purpose for myself."

Later, Taylor found help in the work of Martin Luther, a monk who believed that "no livelihood is dearer to the heart of God than any other. . . . Whatever our jobs in the world happen to be, Luther said, our mutual vocation is to love God and neighbor."[55]

The ways that we express our "mutual vocation"—

loving God and neighbor—vary from one individual to the next, and perhaps it is this diversity that enriches life with color.

I believe that, even in her deafness, Mother heard God. She prayed daily for the departed over holy cards and never missed church. Somewhere along the way, it must have been a calling that led her to the kitchen, for cooking was the way she showed love. Give her a jug of olive oil, a head of garlic, and some fresh basil (which she pronounced buz-lee-gol), and there was no limit to what might appear on the table. In typing this, my fingers itch to yank a leaf of lusciousness from one of her generously stuffed artichokes.

I can still see her floured hands rolling out dough at the yellow laminate table. After cutting zigzag-edged squares and filling them with a ricotta mixture, she would crimp each sack one at a time with a fork, painstakingly creating miniature masterpieces—homemade ravioli. As a young girl watching, I couldn't understand why all the effort for something that would disappear in a couple of swallows.

Soon bored with the endeavor, I was off to my room. There I would stretch out on my bed to write in my journal, compose poetry, or peck away at the old Underwood, creating a family newsletter—*The Vickiville Gazette*—named after my middle sister's firstborn daughter. Or I'd rearrange stuffed animals on my bed and line up framed photos on my dresser, as if anticipating a visit from *House Beautiful* photographers.

It is hard to say why the food I serve takes second billing

to the pattern of my dinnerware. Or why my resumé lists one of my interests as "other people's cooking." Perhaps I wanted to be something more than my mother was, something different. Maybe my being too busy to cook was my hoity-toity way of appearing to have more important things to do.

But late in my mother's life, my husband and I volunteered to prepare a church dinner for eighty-some people. Given the limitations of my own culinary talent, the gesture was partly inane, but mostly an effort to involve Mother in an activity that might revitalize her after my father's death. The evening's entrée was one of her specialties, City Chicken, which isn't what its name implies. It hails from the days when chicken was expensive and features, instead, cubes of pork and veal skewered on a short wooden stick with various stages of dipping and breading, frying and baking.

The minute Mother donned her apron in the church kitchen, she began issuing orders on garlic chopping, breading techniques, and oven temperatures. The stainless steel jungle of double ovens and endless counter space was her Garden of Eden.

That evening, at the conclusion of the meal, our pastor beckoned Mother from the kitchen. At four foot ten, she stood holding a dish towel near the edge of the church hall, a streak of flour across her cheek, as he expressed gratitude for one of the most scrumptious meals ever to come out of the church kitchen. The room shook with thunderous applause. As I watched her suppressing a modest smile, tears of pride welled up inside me. Or maybe they were tears of empathy. Because when it comes to writing—and even my attempts at decorating—there is more than a pinch of my mother in me. My medium may not be food, but like her, I am driven to mix the right ingredients, to achieve a certain flavor.

Each of us, I think, is created with a desire to use our God-given talents to provide a worthwhile experience for others, to give as we are receiving. This is not always an easy thing to do, as witnessed by my struggle with the page. But we yearn for that connection, for that moment of hearing and of feeling heard that is so lucid that we know why we are here.

In a world in which free will is both a blessing and a curse, there are those whose choices get twisted, and the desire to matter is so urgent that, in some cases, it supersedes all else. On December 14, 2012, in Sandy Hook, Connecticut, a gunman decides to take an assault rifle into an elementary school, shooting and killing twenty young children and six members of the staff. On April 15, 2013, at the finish line of the Boston Marathon, two pressure cooker bombs explode, killing three and injuring dozens more—a pair of brothers are suspects.

The outrages rip through the hearts of millions. On many levels, we are baffled, desperate for reassurance that God is among us even in the midst of evil. *Speak to us,* we pray. We've lost touch with God's voice and yearn for the sound of it.

After the tragedies, a quote by the late children's television host Fred Rogers circulates across the Internet: "When I was a boy and I would see scary things in the news, my mother would say to me, 'Look for the helpers. You will always find people who are helping.'"

Victims rise above tragedy in ways that are unfathomable, and in the process, they inspire others. A young dancer who lost a leg in the Boston bombing is determined to dance again. An eighteen-year-old college freshman who was brutally raped by three strangers shares her story in high school and college gymnasiums, offering hope and healing to others, as she moves toward a career as a teacher whom students can trust with their problems. The evils are gut-wrenching, yet the response of these victims and others like them provides inspiration. I think it is what the apostle Paul meant when he praised "the Father of compassion and the God of all comfort, who comforts us in all our troubles, so that we can comfort those in any trouble with the comfort we ourselves receive from God."[56]

To extend one's talents in response to heartache is to answer a sacred calling. From our own pain—whatever the brand of it—compassion arises. And at the juncture of heartache and gift, we sometimes find our mattering.

I see now that my mother's abundant cooking was a way for her to nourish those she loved, to fill them up—she who knew emptiness, she who hungered for love. One of her frequently repeated mantras would come at the end of a bountiful meal. There would be artichokes and city chicken, pasta and meatballs, salad and homemade bread, all served at one sitting. We would feel stuffed as Thanksgiving turkeys, yet for Mother it was never enough.

artichokes & city chicken

"There's more in the kitchen," she'd insist, adamant that no one would leave the table hungry. The gesture hardly seemed to make sense, so extreme was the effort, but perhaps the impetus that drove it was rooted in a pain of long ago. I grasp this now—the intensity of the yearning—as surely as I understand this: Of all the reasons that I write, perhaps the need to feel heard is the truest one.

In *Living a Life That Matters*, Harold S. Kushner tells of the many dying people to whom he has tended in forty years as a rabbi and their varying degrees of fear. "The people who had the most trouble with death were those who felt that they had never done anything worthwhile in their lives," he notes, "and if God would only give them another two or three years, maybe they would finally get it right. It was not death that frightened them; it was insignificance, the fear that they would die and leave no mark on the world."[57]

I remember a white-haired man, years ago, at a bookstore reading. My new book lay closed on the podium, as the audience asked questions. The man sat near the last row of seats, and when he raised his hand, I called on him. He wanted to know how, in *Riding the Dog*, I had described the stories from my father's youth with such specificity. How did I come to acquire the details?

More than a decade before my father died, I explained, I had traveled to my hometown of Pittsburgh specifically to interview him. For three days, we sat at his office desk, a tape recorder between us capturing his stories. Many were familiar to me; with repetition, they'd grown richer. Dad had recently survived quadruple bypass surgery, an event that spurred my interest in preserving the memories in his voice. Other than that, I had no plans for them. After we'd finished, I pushed the "stop" button, and Dad looked across the desk at me.

"You can do anything you want with these," he offered.

Years later, in writing about the final summer of Dad's life, I returned to the tapes and their stories to help paint a picture of him.

The white-haired man in the bookstore looked at me with longing.

"Boy," he said, "I wish someone would ask to hear my stories."

He wanted to feel listened to; he wanted to matter.

This man—whoever he is and wherever he may be—is most likely unaware of the impact that his sentiment has had not only on me, but also on others. For through his yearning, the voice of the Holy Spirit called my name. Later, in a volunteer role, I was to record life stories of hospice patients, an enriching endeavor for me and for them, plus a gift to those they left behind. At the end of life, as they shared their meaningful moments, these people came alive.

The affirmation of our passions, of who we are and what our gifts mean, was aptly described by the late publisher Katharine Graham. "To do what we love and feel that it matters, how can anything be more fun than that?"

Sometimes it seems that the Holy Spirit speaks the-matically to me, as though to drive home a point. Not long after my discovery of the memory book and the reflections it inspired, the phone rings. When I answer it, my friend Mildred, a pastoral care minister, skips the pleasantries of a greeting. She is aware that I've been engaged in an exploration of the Spirit's voice, the spiritual act of listening that leads to finding direction, to calming heartache, to knowing that we are loved. And she is right there with me, championing the cause.

"Did I ever tell you about the email I got from God?" she wants to know. She describes an occasion when she was struggling with self-doubt, a nasty monster rooted in childhood rejection. A belief that her stepmother instilled in her—that there was "something odd" about her contempla-tive stepdaughter and that she was "not the kind of person anyone would ever like"—occasionally plagues Mildred, even in her eighties, and this was one of those times. She wrote an email to one of her sons that detailed a string of unusual happenings she was trying to decipher.

One involved a young man who had approached her after church to tell her that when she was serving the chalice at communion, he suddenly saw her wrapped in a healthy-look-ing green vine. Another of these instances was a dream she'd had, in which she felt as though she were wading through sludge, trying unsuccessfully to climb a staircase. She even-tually called out, "Lord Jesus, help me!" and then she was able to climb more easily.

Finally, on a Tuesday, a twenty-year-old church member

arrived at her office asking if she had a few minutes to give him. The young man asked if a stairway had any meaning to her. Mildred replied that, spiritually, it meant climbing toward God. He then described a vision he'd had in which he'd seen Mildred, all in white, on a stairway. Below the stairs was a gathering of people who were inspired by the way she was climbing. The young man described in detail the exact staircase that had appeared in Mildred's dream: It was straight and made of stone, not very wide, with a wooden railing.

She asked a spiritually gifted priest for his take on the occurrences. The priest told her that perhaps God was telling her that she is a leader.

"Well, I don't feel very much like a leader," she wrote in the email to her son, "and certainly not like any kind of inspiration for anyone, so I still wonder what's going on. I expect the Spirit will let me know."

After typing the last sentence, she glanced at the computer screen, planning to correct any errors. Suddenly, with no strike of keys on her part, the words "I love you" wedged their way into the final sentence and appeared repeatedly to the end of the page, like this:

I expect the S I love you I love you I love you I love you I love you
I love you I love you I love you I love you I love you I love you I
love you I love you I love you I love you I love you I love you I love
you I love you I love you I love you I love you I love you I love you
I love you I love you I love you I love you I love you I love you I
love you I love you I love you I love you I love you I love you I love
you I love you I love you I love you I love you I love you I love you

I love you I love you I love you I love you I love you I love you I
love you I love you I love you I love you I love you I love you I love
you I love you I love you I love you I love you I love you I love you
I love you I love you I love you I love you irit will let me know.

"I have to believe it was the Holy Spirit who interrupted
the email to my son," Mildred tells me. Whatever the
technical explanation, she heard the voice that counts
above all others: that of a Savior who loved each and every
one of us so much that he gave his life for us. How much
more can we matter than that?

—

# My Mother's Zucchini Pie

3 cups zucchini with skin, thinly sliced
4 eggs
1/2 teaspoon salt
1/4 teaspoon pepper
1 teaspoon parsley
1/2 cup oil
1/2 cup Parmesan cheese
1 cup finely chopped onions
1 cup Bisquick

Mix together. Pour into 10" buttered plate.
Bake at 350 degrees for 40–50 minutes.
Check often. It's done when brown on top.

Chapter Six

# wandering and watching

*This is just too much of a coincidence
to be coincidence.*
—Geoff Chester

The writing picks up momentum. A note arrives from Maxine to tell me that every morning at six, she talks to the Lord about me. I picture God bending an ear to hear as she prays me back to my desk. "Chapter One: If a Tree Falls in the Forest." "Chapter Two: Waiting." "Chapter Three: The Discernment Committee." In dawn's early awakening, ideas sashay across my brain. They come to breakfast, join me for prayer, marvel at their own reflection in Bible study. On my tablet all morning, thoughts somersault into words. When a writer is writing, all's right with the world.

But then one day, just like that, there's another stare-down from the page: "Chapter Six." I stop, numb. A sense of urgency presses in. The floodgates open.

*What if I am not the one to write this?*

*What if I get lost?*

*Who will care?*

Years ago, early in his art career, my husband worked as an illustrator. Invariably, people would "oooh" and "aaaah" over his work; clients would return for more, time and again. I remember his drawings of Bill Cosby and Bob Hope for a television poster; the artwork looked more like the celebrities than the stars did themselves.

In spite of these accomplishments, Randy would berate himself. He would drool over the work of Bernie Fuchs, Bart Forbes, and Milton Glaser. He would then convince himself that, in comparison, he simply could not draw. It drove me mad. From an outside perspective, it was hard to comprehend why he wasn't down on his knees in gratitude for the gift of incredible skill. But he felt "like a deer in headlights," he said, and the process sent him spiraling downward, until he was nearly rendered incapable of carrying on. Time after time, he wrestled with this.

I don't know what it is about the human spirit that makes us turn on ourselves, but in some ways, my own trepidation is similar. One moment our gifts seem adequate, even better— and for that, we are grateful—then the next, not so much. Does the Spirit, so kind and generous, suddenly turn stingy? Teasing, taunting—would that be the God of all goodness?

Perhaps the burden is imposed by the misguided notion that everything is up to us, as though our job description has the name of God on it, when really, the load can be so much lighter. The real source of power is right in front of us. But like Peter, we fail to keep our eyes on it, distracted by our own inadequacies.

"Peter got out of the boat, walked on the water, and came toward Jesus. But when he saw the wind, he was afraid and, beginning to sink, cried out, 'Lord, save me!' Immediately,

Jesus reached out his hand and caught him. 'You of little faith,' he said, 'why did you doubt?'"[58]

Like Moses hearing the command to bring the Israelites out of Egypt, we are reluctant—"Who am I, that I should go?"—convinced that surely someone else is more qualified.

Like Paul, we get sidetracked. Early in his journey, he seemed to misunderstand God's will, heading for Asia, then Bythinia where, both times, God stopped and redirected him.

Inherent in our mantras—"I am clueless," "I am inadequate," "I stink at this"—is the root of the problem. The point that needs remembering is that "I" am not the source. With God, good comes out of nothingness—even out of pages refusing to surrender blankness, out of hearts that struggle to hear.

"God can use our detours to get us where he wants us," writes Whitney Kuniholm.[59]

What if the detours are simply ways of being taken aside and addressed with love? What if all that's being asked of me is trust? Perhaps the act of listening means releasing our own agenda. The idea makes sense to me, this impetus to wander and stay open to discoveries that await.

In the spirit of going with the flow—a concept that challenges my take-charge nature—I decide that I could use a break from my work (and vice versa). The frigid December air nips at my gloveless hands as I ring my neighbor's doorbell, holding a tin of cookies. An acquaintance once mentioned that his mother lived several houses away from mine.

I'd intended to introduce myself sooner, but for no good reason, time got away from me.

A shuffle of footsteps approaches the door, a fiddling with the knob, and then through the opening, the chain, still fastened, glistens. A sliver of yellow chenille—Marion's bathrobe—lightens the darkness, as does her silver pixie-cut hair, damp and tousled. Her smile is wide and self-conscious. Acute macular degeneration has left her able to sense movement and the fuzzy shape of a face, but all detail is lost to her.

"I can't let you in," she sings. "I just got out of the shower. Who is it?"

I introduce myself, hand her the tin through the opening.

"You sound like you're young enough to be my granddaughter!" Her voice is throaty and confident. "Will you come back again?"

"Yes, definitely. Sorry I didn't call first. I will next time."

"No, no, it's fine. I like surprises," she offers. "And I'd love to talk to you."

The holidays come and go, busy for both of us. Finally, we arrange a date for tea at her house, which she refers to as "an off-campus retirement cottage," while mine, she says, is more of the Hansel and Gretel variety. When I arrive, sunlight streams through the bay window, warming her living room.

"Dear, I am sure you are beautiful," she says, "but I can't see you."

She takes my coat and opens the closet door. There is no sign of an empty hanger—the closet is full. Marion's hands move swiftly along the rod, until finally, in the back, she reaches one. In the kitchen, she pours boiling water from a kettle into a teapot, estimating in increments the number of cups.

"There," she says. "Is it filled?"

I look into the teapot.

"About halfway."

"Okay, tell me when it's two-thirds filled." She continues pouring. Then her fingers dance across the countertop, opening tins, taking out cookies and chocolate-dipped dates and arranging them on a platter. She fills a bowl with mixed nuts and then invites me to choose the teabags—three of them, to make it plenty strong. After the tea has steeped, she pours it into cups.

She loads the snacks onto a tray, allowing me only to carry the tea—she can manage the rest—and we head to the family room where cushioned chairs overlook the wooded backyard.

She purchased this bungalow years ago with input from family and friends, she tells me, then acclimated herself to the positions of her belongings. It was time to downsize, and she wasn't ready to enter a retirement community.

"I didn't want to be surrounded by old people," she says, smiling, "like me."

Marion and I chat for more than two hours, the conversation lively. The timeliness of our meeting strikes me; her perseverance speaks clearly. For just as I am losing my way—the writing stalled, the voice stifled—here comes this vibrant woman, nearly blind, who has managed to find hers.

"There are no mistakes, no coincidences," according to psychiatrist and author Elisabeth Kübler-Ross, a pioneer in studies on death and dying. "All events are blessings given to us to learn from."

Research shows that the term "coincidence"was probably coined by a Medieval Latinist, and was later to be appropriated by mathematicians to represent a well-known geometrical concept. The word is derived from the Latin *cum* (meaning "with," "together") and *incidere* (a composed verb from *"in"* and *"cadere"*: "to fall on," "to happen"). Wikipedia defines it as "an event notable for its occurring in conjunction with other conditions, e.g. another event. As such, a coincidence occurs when something uncanny, accidental and unexpected happens."

"Coincidence," wrote Albert Einstein, "is God's way of remaining anonymous."

The first example of the word discovered in English, in Sir Matthew Hale's *Moral Essays*, referred to "a coincidence of two great matters, namely, the day of the resurrection and the day of the mission of the Holy Spirit."[60] Is this in itself coincidental, that the first known application of the word in English was a sacred one? The day of the resurrection and the day of the mission of the Holy Spirit! Was it merely a fluke that these two events coincided?

A different word, *synchronicity,* embraced by philosophers such as Carl Jung, refers to the occurrence of two or more events that have no apparent relevance to one another, but still have significant correlation.

In *The Celestine Prophecy*, James Redfield and Carol Adrienne share the story of Elisabeth Kübler-Ross, who described a turning point while she was working in a residency with Dr. Sydney Margolin. Kübler-Ross remembered working on a polygraph machine one day when Dr. Margolin came in, saying he had to go somewhere, and asked her to take over his lectures.

"This was like replacing God!" she said. "I died a thousand deaths. . . ."

Advised to choose any subject dealing with psychiatry, Kübler-Ross felt that the students should know about death and dying, so she went to the library to research what had been written about it. When she got there, she was surprised by the dearth of material.

Redfield and Adrienne note that "perhaps her choice of subject was unknowingly shaped by her early experiences in war relief in Europe, from which she still carries the images of those who perished in death camps. Or perhaps this was a point of divine intervention. Whatever guided her choice of subject that day, Kübler-Ross's initial lecture on death and dying started a chain of events that changed the direction of her life and opened up what turned out to be a life's mission."[61]

Meeting Marion was a revitalizing send-off to the Treehouse, where Randy and I are taking in the serenity. The fireplace warms our little getaway, quiet and still. It is Saturday morning. The tea is room temperature. My husband and I have been chatting, oblivious to time. My mind starts to wander, and I am half-listening, half-looking out the window. Mountains rise in the distance, a captivating view. I barely notice when he stands and leaves the room.

Tucked away for now is the manuscript with which I've been struggling. When it turned into a battle of the wills—the work's versus mine—it occurred to me that we both needed to breathe, to have space and time to ourselves, sending me on reprieve. In the hollow my work left behind, I made a new friend in Marion, who was close to the age Mother had reached. There was nothing else like her except their impairments—one of sight, the other of hearing. Now, like the fire's flickering flames, memories of Mother have been reignited.

It is as if, once again, I am standing next to the hospital bed where she lies wild-eyed and panic-stricken. She has been admitted after falling and breaking a hip, then transferred to intensive care for a respiratory issue. In the process, they have taken away her hearing aids.

She struggles to talk, but her words are garbled. I try to understand. She pushes at the oxygen mask, guttural sounds echoing. Her mouth is dry. Does she need water? I offer her the straw. She shakes her head no. An indentation from the mask's pressure marks the crook of her nose. Is the mask too tight? I loosen it, but again, she indicates no. Her expression is deflated as though I don't get it, as though I never will. The guessing gets us nowhere; it never has. What is the source of her angst? What is it that she wants? What does she need? For God's sake, what does my mother need?

Finally, she leans her head to the side and escapes into a deep sleep from which nothing can awaken her, not my sister's and my prodding, not the doctors' loud voices, not a visit from her out-of-town granddaughter. Days pass. And at last, on her own, she awakens. Again, the agitation, the unintelligible speech. And in me, the helplessness. The pattern is familiar: an unnamed pain felt by Mother, my attempts to assuage it, my failure to do so.

On a humid August morning, the hospital halls are tranquil. It seems that Mother is the only patient in intensive care. Around the corner, I approach her room, and there she lies, her paper-thin skin bruised from injections. In her eyes, a look of defeat says that she is finished begging. To my surprise, black bands are tied around her bony wrists and strapped to the bed rails, holding her captive. I shoot out to the nurses' station.

"She kept trying to yank off the respirator in the middle of the night," the nurse explains, "and to get out of bed."

"I need you to take off the straps," I say. "Now."

The mountains outside the Treehouse window stand stalwart, unmovable, as the memory tumbles through my heart, seeping into every crack and crevice of my being. The shackles haunt me, reminders of that which tied Mother down, keeping her away. I may never know the full story of her pain; I don't even know if I could bear it or if she would want me to. But in my heart, I know that my mother loved me. Could the distance between us have been armor, a way for her to protect me from whatever issues may have bound her? They were problems that had nothing to do with me or my failure to mitigate them—I am sure of this now—for their seeds, I believe, took root long before my existence.

Within days, at a nearby hospice facility, my mother died.

Whatever plagues us on Earth, we are told, will be taken away in Heaven. There is no sickness or trouble or pain. Any difficulties suffered will be turned to our advantage, helping us to become" mature and complete, not lacking anything."[62]

Through God's grace, there are new glimpses of the woman who gave birth to me. They arrive by way of the Spirit, who seems to have designated three different messengers: Maxine, Mildred, and Marion. The encouragement, the compassion, the warmth. My mother, and someday, myself. I can only imagine our reunion.

The hills are snow covered, frosting on cupcakes. Twenty-eight degrees on a winter morning. Sunlight streams through the window. The pencil in my hand casts a shadow upon the page. And, at last, words appear where before there was only blankness. Gratitude fills me.

Jesus walked the Earth. He listened. He watched, taking note of the lilies of the field. And he shared parables. A friend tells me that my efforts at writing remind him of what Jesus did—the wandering, the watching, the sharing. His words give me hope. I dwell in the thought, longing to do justice to it, yearning to be worthy, but of course I am not. My Creator knows this, and I know it, and that is why gifts from God are called grace.

Even the doubts that I have harbored (*Who am I to share stories? Who will care?*) are addressed. My bed is cozy as I curl up to read a Frederick Buechner memoir. Propped-up pillows cushion my neck, cotton jersey softness soothes my skin. The book rests open at my waist, and there in black and white on page one are the musings of a gifted and prolific author, harboring misgivings about writing of an autobiographical nature, the same issue that's been pressing on my own mind.

"It is like telling somebody in detail how you are before they have asked the question, How are you? Indeed, it isn't like it; it is it. But I do it anyway because I need to do it. After forty years of writing books, I find I need to put things into words before I can believe that they are entirely real."[63]

The timing is perfect, the voice of compassion. Nothing is wasted, not even the detours. I think of the apostle Paul amid unimaginable suffering: the insults, the persecution, the flogging, the stoning, the imprisonment, the shipwreck, the hunger, the thirst, the cold, the nakedness. Detours, to be sure, but to Paul, they were stepping-stones drawing him closer to the source of strength.

"I delight in weaknesses . . . in hardships . . . in difficulties," he wrote. "For when I am weak, then I am strong."[64]

## My Mother's Bon Bon Cookies

2 cups flour
1/2 teaspoon baking soda
1/2 cup shortening
1 cup brown sugar
1/2 cup sour milk
2 squares melted chocolate
1/2 cup chopped nuts
1/4 teaspoon salt
1 teaspoon vanilla

Mix baking soda and flour together.
Add all other ingredients, and mix well.
Drop by teaspoons on cookie sheet. Bake at 350
for 10 or 12 minutes only. Let cool.
Icing:
    2 tablespoons margarine
    1-3/4 cups powdered sugar
    2 tablespoons canned milk
    1 square chocolate
    1 teaspoon vanilla
    1/4 teaspoon salt
Mix all together and frost.

# the unfathomable character of life

*You shall see wonders.*
—William Shakespeare

"So you lather your hands and rub them together in a downward motion, like this." The volunteer coordinator stands at the kitchen sink, water running, in this wing of the Essa Flory Center that used to be the hospice inpatient unit. "Make sure to get between the fingers and under the fingernails."

Gatherings of volunteers and staff parade from one station to the next, chattering in the hall onto which the kitchen opens. This facility is now used as doctors' offices and for training like that of tonight, primarily for new volunteers, though, for me, it's a refresher required after a respite from service.

"Do this for at least twenty seconds," the coordinator advises, "or the equivalent of singing two rounds of 'Happy Birthday.'"

Years ago, between vigils at Mother's bedside across the

hall—she was in room number four, I remember—my sisters and I shared take-out meals in this kitchen. The hall was quiet then, the space sacred. Now the absence of the dying feels profound. Though at times my mother would kick off the bed covers, she was also as calm here as I'd ever seen her. I push away memories, not wanting to deal with emotion.

After the hand-washing demonstration, trainees are split into groups of four. We are led to various rooms where nurses wait to teach us how to transfer a patient from bed to wheelchair and back again. My role does not require this skill, so I am advised that I'll just be observing. The volunteer coordinator ushers my group toward a room, and when I see which one—room number four—I feel my heart tighten.

It hasn't changed in all these years. There are French doors leading out to a patio, a breakfast nook where we parked purses, the bookshelves on which I once placed flowers and family photos. The bed still juts out from the right-hand wall, facing the brown leather sofa where my sisters and I sat, waiting, where I remember trying to sleep at night, listening for Mother's breathing.

Now I am the only one in my particular group who is simply observing, and the training nurse singles me out.

"Would you be willing to play the role of the patient?" she asks.

I nod and smile, though inside I am cringing. I crawl into the bed, trying not to display awkwardness, trying not to freak at the eeriness, trying not to question why God would want me propped in what once was Mother's deathbed. Somewhere beyond, the nurse's words float—instructions on wheel locks, adjusting the footrests, where to place the patient's shoes—but at this very moment, here we are, my mother and I, united in oneness through the view of a brown leather sofa, a spot of rest for those who will someday seek peace.

Philosopher Milton Mayeroff writes of the "unfathomable character of life" as gift, "something to savor, like the wonder in looking up at the stars at night. Like wonder," he suggests, "it is something to undergo, to realize and to appreciate, the mystery of existence itself, the mystery and amazement that anything exists at all."[66]

With God as "the author of life," is there any wonder that the character of our existence would be unfathomable?

My journey of listening guides me through myriad stops of wonder. At this particular junction, reminders of the unfathomable character of life return to me. Memories of soothing moments, so full of surprise, reveal the presence of sacred voice.

*I am with you,* God says through the remembrances. *I have always been with you.*

I think back to the day that Randy and I first left Katherine at college. It was muggy in Brooklyn, the air closing in, making it hard to breathe. The van was unpacked, the neighborhood explored, and now it was time to be on our way. We huddled with our younger daughter, hugging good-bye behind the freshman dorm. Like a divine show of empathy, a crack of thunder followed by a hard, driving downpour descended onto the parking lot. I do not remember whether or not we held an umbrella, but either way, our faces were drenched.

On the way home, the van, earlier filled with boxes, clothing, camera equipment, bedding, and stuffed animals, now echoed with emptiness.

The day after Randy and I returned home, I approached the garage for a trip to the grocery store. To the right side of the flagstone walkway, two butterflies flitted in circles, bumping into one another as though they were lost, not unlike the state in which my husband and I found ourselves. Having forgotten the grocery list, I hurried back into the house. Upon my return, there on the other side of the path was a smaller butterfly, all by itself, soaring skyward. I stopped in awe to watch it. Like the butterfly, my daughter was off with great purpose to accomplish something. (Who else but the Spirit would whisper a thought so tender?)

Now a rising junior, she is facing logistical challenges regarding a summer internship in the city. I keep telling myself to trust the Divine Caretaker, but then a scammer tries to bilk her out of her room rent, and a pair of boxing gloves in a tiny corner of my heart puts their dukes up. A laundry list of potential problems arise. She is capable of handling details, but I am inclined to take charge. And then a white-on-white pattern of butterflies on a nearby curtain reminds me that this is all part of her spreading her wings. How lovely and true is the voice that I hear!

Metaphor is one of God's languages of love. It is a way that the Holy Spirit takes us aside to offer affirmation. Things will work out, not necessarily according to our own plan, but an even better one.

"Without metaphor," poses author and hospice counselor Eve Joseph, "how could we understand the man on his deathbed who tells you a yellow cab has pulled up outside his house, and even though the taxi has the wrong address, he says he'll go anyway?"[65]

Without metaphor, how would we find hope as we wander through heartache? Metaphor provides meaning. It deepens understanding. It connects one Truth to another. Like a mother's first gaze into her newborn's eyes, it triggers revelation: There *has* to be a God. There *are* miracles.

As my daughter is moving away from me, my mother returns, dawdling in the back of my mind. She has followed me to Maxine's, shared stillness in the mountains and a view from a hospice bed. The more tuned in I am to the voice that resurrects her, the more my heart soars. Perhaps this, too, is a message of the butterfly—the promise that there is still hope for change.

One afternoon several years ago, I bumped into an old friend and former client, whom I hadn't seen in years, at an office-supply store. We spoke, and he shared the news that his forty-five-year-old wife had died four years earlier in a car crash.

I was stunned, nearly speechless.

"How did you make it through?" I asked.

"It was faith," Clair said without hesitation. He had no idea that I'd just finished a project that explored grief from a faith perspective; the first shipment of newly printed books had arrived at my home that very morning. "Things happened that led me to recognize the hand of God and Beth in offering comfort."

"Like what?"

He described a birthday trip he and his wife had taken from Pennsylvania to their vacation home in Hilton Head, South Carolina. Unbeknownst to Clair, Beth had invited friends from home to travel ahead and surprise him. She had given them the house key so that they would be there when she and Clair arrived.

After they landed at the Savannah airport, she secretly called their friends to inform them of Clair's and her impending arrival. But Beth never made it. On their way, a car ran a red light and crashed into the rental that they were driving, killing her immediately. Later that night, Clair sat in a vehicle with a state trooper. Her name, he noted on her nametag, was "Angel."

"Is there someone you would like to call?" Angel asked.

"No. It's almost midnight, and there's nothing anyone can do anyway. I'll wait until morning," he said. "Plus, there's something wrong with my cell phone—it's not working."

"Here, let me see that thing," Angel said. She took the phone and shook it, accidentally pushing the speed dial number that connected to the cell phone of Clair's best friend. His friend answered, and Angel handed the phone to Clair.

"What's going on?" the friend wanted to know.

"There's been an accident," Clair explained.

"Where are you? I'll be right there."

"No, you don't understand. I'm down in Hilton Head."

"Yes, I know," said the friend. "So am I."

"You are?"

Within minutes, Clair's closest friend was by his side.

Later, at the funeral, participants stepped out of church into the Lancaster County sunlight—more than a hundred miles from any seashore—and there flying overhead, as though in a grand gesture of tribute to Beth and the beach she had loved, was a flock of seagulls.

As I stood in the store listening to my friend's story, my heart ached for him. At the same time, it was clear that the miracle of grace, through faith, had embraced him. In the darkest throes of sorrow, he'd heard the love of God's voice.

Later, with Clair's consent, I conveyed his story to audiences at book talks. Through his sharing, others who grieved found comfort in recognizing the presence of a God who weeps with us, the God who stands beside us.

The sequence of events surpassed the possibility of human endeavor: the tragedy of loss, the grace that helped see a survivor through, a chance meeting in a store, audiences touched by hope. Unfathomable.

The arrival of a divine voice in the heart is so varied in its form of transportation that it is difficult to categorize. One moment, the whisper is detected in the flight of a butterfly, another in a flock of seagulls, and still another from the fourth row of wooden chairs in a bookstore gathering.

On a mild spring evening, I returned to my hometown

of Pittsburgh to do a reading. My notes were on the podium. A few crafters who met regularly at the bookstore sat off to the side, knitting, tatting, crocheting. Other than the crafters, I believe I would have been able to attach a name to each face I saw: aunts and uncles, cousins, nieces, grandnieces, great-grandnephews, an old high school friend and her husband.

One might expect reassurance from an audience of familiar faces, but a jittery feeling caught me off guard. I breathed in a prayer, *Help me, God.* Suddenly, from the fourth row of folding chairs, my Aunt Mary's voice broke the silence.

"Is somebody going to give a speech?" she piped up. My book talk, it's safe to assume, was the first such event she'd attended in her eighty-some years. An overwhelming sense of gratitude comforted me. I leaned toward the microphone.

"I love you, Aunt Mary," I said.

"I love you, too, Janny," she called out.

It had been decades since I'd been called by that name. In the eyes of God, just as in those of our doting aunts, we are precious. Our concerns are God's concerns. Like relatives in large Italian clans, our Creator is there for us. Like the lace created by the tatter's needle, the weaving is intricate.

*I love you, God.*

*I love you, too, Janny.*

The nickname takes me back to my growing-up years, enriched by dozens of family members, generous with love. There was a bend-over-backwards effort to lend support, not just to me but to others, as well: neighbors unable to afford groceries at my grandparents' store who were supplied with them anyway; orphans welcomed into our homes; entire classes of high school students invited for spaghetti dinner. Aunts, uncles, great-aunts, great-uncles were always nearby, treating us kids as their own.

In the Gospel of Matthew, we are referred to as "the salt of the earth . . . the light of the world."[68]

In the Gospel of John, Jesus says, "I lay down my life for the sheep."[69] The sheep, of course, symbolize all of us.

In 1 John, we are reminded, "See what great love the Father has lavished on us, that we should be called children of God! And that is what we are!"[70]

The Psalmist petitions God to "keep me as the apple of your eye."[71]

Metaphor can be an expression of sacred endearment, generously bestowed in Scripture and in our lives.

In her role as pastoral care minister, Mildred has held hands with the addicted and comforted the dying. In more than eight decades on Earth, she has learned to find peace. But on this particular evening—smack dab in the middle of my wrestling match with the muse, as well as pressing personal matters—she is also feeling overwhelmed. Our prayer group is meeting at her house. The space heater whirs in the sitting room where we gather, bundled in sweaters and scarves to stay warm. Mildred, whose internal thermometer is perennially set higher than that of the rest of us, fans the heat from her face. Her cat, Micah, is curled on her lap.

Mildred is sharing a variety of pressures that she has felt mounting. Then she mentions a sign she saw in front of a local church: "Repeat after me: I am too blessed to feel stressed."

"I have one thing to say about that," she asserts. "Bullshit."

I love it when God stoops down to meet me where I am. It gives me hope that there is a way out of it.

When Jesus sent his twelve disciples into the ripe fields "to tenderly care for the bruised and hurt lives," he told them not to "worry about what you'll say or how you'll say it. The right words will be there; the Spirit of your Father will supply the words."[72]

*Please, Father, supply the words.*

My printer spits out draft after draft of my work-in-progress, this dogged attempt to turn up the volume of God's voice. Where is this leading? The more insistent I am about seeing beyond the moment, the less trust I display. Writing is like a mystery unfolding. It has been said that it happens away from the desk just as much as it does at it. The effort requires abandon. So I take a break, a walk, a swim. I run errands.

At a gift shop, a green and red greeting card with white balloons celebrates a new birth. I'm not looking for a baby card, but this one seems to know exactly what has been on my mind, this idea of Mayeroff's—the unfathomable character of life. The Shakespeare quote on the front of the card reaches across centuries.

"You shall see wonders."

The timing is precise, the voice clear. *Keep going. Stay the course. Believe.*

# My Mother's Eggplant

1 egg*
1/4 teaspoon black pepper
1 eggplant, sliced thin, lengthwise
oregano
Mix together:
1 cup bread crumbs
1/2 cup grated Italian cheese
1 clove chopped garlic
chopped fresh parsley, to taste

Beat egg and black pepper together.
Dip eggplant in egg, then in bread crumb
mixture.
Deep fry in oil. Drain on paper towels.
Lay in layers in oblong dish.
Sprinkle oregano lightly between layers.
Can be served hot or cold.

* My sister questions whether one egg is enough for a
  whole eggplant. This is a recipe that my mother learned
  from her mother, so I won't fiddle with it, but you're
  welcome to use as many eggs as needed.

Chapter Eight

# drinking the water

*We get to Heaven, not by what we achieve,
but what we yearn for, I think.*
—Gerald Shapiro

Indian summer—heated and vicious—chokes the air. At times, my journey through silence has been like this—stifling, oppressive. The pedals on my bike feel like blocks of cement, the pebbles on the path like boulders. A novice biker, concerned about having to stop who-knows-where to pee, I purposely didn't eat or drink anything before the four of us headed onto the Great Allegheny Passage. I am about to learn a lesson in staying hydrated.

The humidity dampens my brow and gives me piggy fingers, though the others seem unaffected. Randy and my friend Marilyn speed ahead side by side, chatting and gaining distance. David, Marilyn's husband, rides slightly behind me. The eighteen-mile Big Savage Tunnel round trip was Marilyn and David's idea, a journey they'd taken before. Randy and I were game, even though our bicycle wheels were laced with spider webs, not used in years.

With the zeal of a tour guide, David is filling me in on the history of the tunnel. Originally built to accommodate the passage of trains through the mountains, it was recently restored, a painstaking endeavor that took two years and twelve million dollars to complete. With its reopening, hikers and bikers can now make an uninterrupted 141-mile journey from Pittsburgh to Cumberland, Maryland.

About a mile from Meyersdale, where we started, we cross an old railroad bridge, the waters of the Youghiogheny rushing below our path, and I am barely able to breathe. David shares details about the old railway line, and I want to express gratitude or, at least, make polite listening noises, but this is not possible. My energy is waning, and I need every ounce of it just to keep pedaling. Finally, David rides alongside me. He glances at my face, then looks again.

"Why don't we stop for water?" he suggests, which is so much kinder than *you look like you're ready to keel over*, which surely he must be thinking.

Yes, I manage to nod.

From my red face, wobbly knees, and parched throat, it takes little time for the others to figure out what is wrong with me. Without a hint of judgment, Marilyn and David extol the virtues of hydration. They sit beside the path as I down water, then half a sandwich, breathing and breathing. It is all that is needed to revive me. I decide to return to the car so the three of them can continue toward the tunnel, but they refuse, insisting instead that we regroup to embark on a shorter route there.

"One for all, and all for one," David asserts.

The four of us head back to the car together, load the bikes, and drive to a parking area closer to our destination.

We pick up the trail again, humidity pressing, occasionally stopping to rehydrate. Finally, Big Savage welcomes us, a mile-long cavern of mistiness, ten degrees cooler than the path that brought us here.

Inside, thirty-two bulletproof lights dot the ceiling. Our voices bounce off the tunnel's walls. Relief. The pedaling is easy, feet moving rhythmically, whole body wheeling, in tune. We ride, refreshed, toward the daylight and, finally, out into it. And there, around the curve, gathered proud as a family portrait, the trees of three states—Pennsylvania, Maryland, and West Virginia—meet in a mountainous embrace. Green against green, tree against tree, leaf against leaf. In a figurative sense this time, the vista takes my breath away. We clutch the brakes, drop our kickstands, and sit on a nearby bench. I do not want to leave. Drinking the water was a minor investment to reap the reward of all this magnificence.

"Come near to God, and he will come near to you."[73]

If the writing—or life itself, for that matter—flowed easily without any tension, there would be no discovery, no chance to come out the other end of the tunnel and behold what we never knew existed. Immersion, I'm finding, is key. Not that it conjures supernatural powers, but it allows them in, enriching the voyage.

One definition of immersion is "baptism in which the whole body of the person is submerged in the water." Another is "the state of being deeply engaged; absorption."[74] The process of discerning sacred voice is like that, an act of immersion, a baptism of sorts. As in the sacrament, a dedication takes place—and the greater the commitment, the sharper the ability to hear.

Decades ago, when I did a stint as a local newspaper correspondent, the assignments that landed on my desk often led me into uncharted waters, and I dove in. In immersion, when applied in the journalistic sense, the writer commits to do research and interview others about the subject at hand. An experiential component might also be involved, a direct engagement in an activity for the purpose of becoming better informed about it.

The antique baskets of a collector I interviewed appealed to my penchant for the old, and soon, amid musty-smelling aisles of flea markets, a basket collection of my own took shape. A couple I interviewed about a marriage encounter program exuded romance, and before long, suitcases were packed for my then husband and me to engage in a weekend of learning to "dialogue." A duo of hairstylists raved about the new, shorter hairstyles that were coming into vogue, and just like that, I was sitting in one of their salon chairs with inches of my shoulder-length hair cascading to the floor.

Immersion engages hearts and minds; however, distractions are plentiful, waiting to trip us up and trigger chaos. Just like the antique baskets that are now scattered who-knows-where, just like the marriage that, in spite of the encounter, ended in divorce, just like the hair that grew out and needed restyling, the commitment to hear a spiritual voice requires constant renewal and repeated replenishment. A few months after the bike trip, the subject of staying hydrated is again brought to my attention.

Lights flash, zigzagging across screens, punching holes in night's darkness, as an emergency-room gurney supports my weary body. Glucose is pumped into my veins, alleviating dehydration triggered by some crazy midnight event, featuring dizziness, nausea, blacking out on the way to or from the bathroom, I do not remember which. They poke; they prod; they test—oh, please let me sleep. In the end, I learn two things.

First, my vagus nerve has tripped.

"Where's that?" I ask. The ER doctor towers over me, dark ponytail, black-rimmed glasses, woolly beard.

"It's in your body," he says. Apparently, he is serious. I shudder, a tiny bit concerned over who has been assigned to the graveyard shift. Later, I look up the term. *Vagus* is derived from Latin and means "wandering." The nerve wanders from the brain stem through organs in the neck, thorax, and abdomen. A wanderer, restless—okay, God, I hear you— like me. No one has an explanation of what instigated the problem, but in the process, my blood pressure took a nose-dive, necessitating the intravenous glucose feeding.

Second, I learn that water consumption helps to raise blood pressure, and that should the symptoms return, $H_2O$ is the way to go. Again, the reminder to stay hydrated. Another nudge from the Holy Spirit? In an effort to continue the conversation, I turn to the Bible.

The water metaphor appears repeatedly in Scripture, especially throughout the Old Testament. It reflects the unique nourishment offered by our Creator, the kind that satisfies the soul's desire. We encounter God as "the spring of living water,"[75] "the fountain of life."[76] The invitation, "Come, all you who are thirsty, come to the waters,"[77] promises refreshment, soothing the yearning soul.

My craving to hear and to be heard, my very parchedness, is being offered a fountain that can fill it full. God wants to be the source of our nourishment. Yet even if we accept the invitation, hydration is not a once-and-done process. Just as the body needs replenishment, the spirit and soul need to be revitalized. We may pride ourselves on having risen to the standard, but when the standard is Jesus, there is a long way to go. The reminders keep coming—again and again and again.

Back from the Treehouse, I return to my desk. An email pops into my in-box. It was sent to a long list of names, including mine, and attached is a newly produced brochure. It comes from a well-respected businessman who, as a volunteer, oversaw the booklet's production and has every right to feel proud of it. But I, as self-appointed Czarina of Creativity, see improvements to be made and know just the person to make them. I forward the piece to my graphic designer husband, suggesting the project as a new business opportunity. The message I attach notes that Randy "could up the quality of it big time!!!" Not one but three exclamation points. And you can guess the rest.

Instead of clicking the "forward" button, the Czarina, in a stroke reflecting pathetically lacking technical skills, sends the unsolicited critique directly to the gentleman who was so eager to share. In spite of his gracious acceptance of my apology—and perhaps because of it—the Czarina feels knocked to her knees.

The message I hear is clear. Letting go requires leaving my pride at the hatcheck. It means acknowledging that the One who placed the moon and the stars in the sky, who formed mountains and carved streams, who created man from dust and woman from a rib bone, might have just a tiny bit more expertise in running the world than I do. My friend Kim once recalled her own reticence to relinquish control.

"I used to think I had all the answers," she said, "that I was all that and a bag of potato chips." In many ways, I am right there with Kim; in others, I am still working on the "used to" part.

The voice persists, the one that whispers, "Hand it over." It waits for us to pay attention, but often we are confused or lost, anxious or too damned full of ourselves. It waits with endless patience, even with loving kindness, if only we will listen. Faith cannot play a role unless we let it.

Now, on the first Sunday of Advent, my deacon friend Janie is giving the sermon. She talks about Jesus destroying the merchants' tables outside of the temple. She suggests that an effort in tearing down may be needed in the process of waiting for that which is coming and most worthwhile.

"What temples need to be destroyed?" she asks. "What false temples have we built between God and ourselves that are obstructing the relationship?"

"I know what mine are," she offers. "What are yours?"

*Pride*, I answer silently. The knowledge is as clear as anything I have ever heard. The struggles on the page, the failed connections. Here in the quiet of Sunday's service, I stand before God, and the only thing I can say is *Help me.*

Now at the passing of the peace, I turn and, though this is rarely the case, the person who happens to be standing next to me is my friend Kim.

"I used to think I had all the answers . . . "

We hug and express our love for one another. God's mercy is abundantly clear.

We don't have all the answers; we won't ever have them, barely even a tiny portion of them. The good news is that our Creator knows all that needs grasping. The mysteries belong to God. All we need to do is be still and know who God is.

"If I can stay calm, faithful, and unconfused while in the middle of the turmoil of life, the goal of the purpose of God is being accomplished in me," writes Oswald Chambers. "What people call preparation God sees as the goal itself."[78]

The process itself is the goal. The drinking of the water, the staying hydrated, the letting go, the listening, the trust, the embrace of each moment—sorrow and all—peaceful in the faith that God is in charge. This is immersion. In being lost, to feel in step with the One who knows the way; in being alone, to feel safe in God's arms; in doing wrong, to accept forgiveness. This is the peace of God, which transcends all understanding.[79]

A new morning. Still resting on my pillow, I sense a whisper. Thoughts tap at my mind's door; the Spirit speaks tenderly now, with inspiration that I did not know I was seeking. Ideas swirl. They gain traction, and start to build on one another. A flurry of excitement. Is this the prompt toward new work?

Help me to serve you, Father. Please tell me how.

"I will show you the most excellent way," Scripture answers.[80]

"Love is patient, love is kind. It does not envy, it does not boast, it is not proud. It does not dishonor others, it is not self-seeking, it is not easily angered, it keeps no record of wrongs. Love does not delight in evil but rejoices with the truth. It always protects, always trusts, always hopes, always perseveres."[81]

How does faith play a role?

The pastor's long-ago question lit a journey's path, continues to light it. It is so enormous that each day there are new revelations. Even in deafening silence, we can learn to hear. Even amid noisy clutter, our Father's voice is steady and true. The discovery then is this: By the grace of God, faith doesn't merely play a role in the work; faith *is* the work. It takes life beyond being livable, providing what no other work, in any amount, can offer: the peace of knowing that we are never forgotten, never abandoned, always forgiven, and always loved. Faith is its own sacred calling. It is work that replenishes itself. And thankfully, there is much of it left to do.

## My Mother's Peanut Butter Fudge

2 cups sugar

1 small can evaporated milk

1 jar marshmallow (7-1/2 oz.)

1 jar peanut butter (12 oz.)

Cook sugar and milk together for three minutes.
Remove from stove, fold in marshmallow and
peanut butter.
Do not beat; just keep turning with spoon.
Pour in buttered pan.
Let set until firm, then score and cut.

# the moravian trombone choir

*First go and be reconciled to them;*
*then come and offer your gift.*
—Matthew 5:24

My friend Nan calls me a church whore. I wander from sanctuary to chapel to meetinghouse, searching. Now in this season of Lent, amid my ongoing efforts to listen, I have taken up a practice of worship at whatever service I can find on each of the forty days. Many of the churches are new to me. I do this not so much out of piety, but out of hopefulness. Reconciliation is like that. The gestures to make—*I am sorry, I forgive you, I forgive myself*—are right in front of our eyes, yet we think there must be some other unturned stone, so we keep on looking, fervently expectant.

It is Ash Wednesday. The car's navigation system leads to a country lane bordered by horse fencing, a blush of sun softening February's bite. At a T in the road, a tiny stone chapel stands off to the left, quaint, charming. I make the turn. Oh, I hope that is it. And it is. Hope Church.

Inside, ten congregants gather. Our voices rise in praise. Ashes to ashes, dust to dust. A stained-glass portrayal of Jesus draped in a white and red robe hangs at the rear of the altar. His hands are outstretched as if to say, *Come. Come abide in me. Come lean on me. Come follow me. You don't even have to name your sorrows; I already know.* My shoulders relax, and though this is my first visit here, my heart feels at home.

Embedded in the side wall, a memorial stone commemorates the life of a woman named Mary Grubb, born October 12, 1816, died March 8, 1900. Later, I learn that the building was erected as the chapel of the Grubb family, the original owners of the nearby mansion and its surrounding acres. The verse inscribed under the name of the deceased pays tribute of the noblest sort: "Blessed are the pure of heart." Later at my desk, the words will return like a whisper from the Spirit, to remind me:

Blessed are the poor in spirit,
for theirs is the kingdom of heaven.
Blessed are those who mourn,
for they will be comforted.
Blessed are the meek,
for they will inherit the earth.
Blessed are those who hunger and thirst
for righteousness,
for they will be filled.
Blessed are the merciful,
for they will be shown mercy.
Blessed are the pure in heart,
for they will see God.
Blessed are the peacemakers,
for they will be called children of God. . . . [82]

The promises offer hope, God's loving assurance that Mother has been comforted; Mother has been shown mercy; Mother has been filled; Mother knows Heaven. And so will I.

Now, at the sign of peace, congregants weave in and out of pews, greeting one another, most often with a handshake. One woman hugs me. After the service, as I cross the street to the parking lot, she hurries to catch up to me.

"I hope you don't mind that I hugged you," she says.

"Not at all," I say. "We all need hugs."

The sweetness of connection. How we yearn for it.

God speaks with the voice of forgiveness in the story of Joseph in Genesis. In listening, we learn that good can come even from mistakes—our own and those of others—however grave they may have been. Forgiveness doesn't render mistakes harmless; it simply lifts the burden and frees the heart to find peace.

Joseph endured hardship at the hands of his own brothers. They threw him into a cistern. They sold him as a slave. Later, he was falsely accused of sexual impropriety when, in fact, what he had done was the right thing. He was thrown into jail. Because of his ability to interpret dreams—a gift he credited to God—he was eventually brought before the Pharaoh King of Egypt.

The symbolism in one of Pharaoh's dreams struck Joseph as a message that there would be seven years of abundance followed by seven years of famine, so he advised Pharaoh to store up grain in the good times to prepare for the bad.

Pharaoh was so grateful for this insight that he placed Joseph in charge of the palace.

"When the famine had spread . . . Joseph opened the storehouses. . . . And all the world came to Egypt to buy grain from Joseph, because the famine was severe everywhere."[83]

And this, after many years, was the occasion that brought ten of Joseph's brothers face to face with him once again. Joseph recognized his brothers, who had come to purchase grain, but they did not recognize him. Finally, when he revealed his identity, the brothers were terrified.

"Do not be distressed and do not be angry with yourselves for selling me here," Joseph told them, "because it was to save lives that God sent me ahead of you . . . to preserve for you a remnant on earth and to save your lives by a great deliverance."[84]

Forgiveness at its finest.

"The mass is ended," says the priest. "Go in peace to glorify the Lord by your life."

"Thanks be to God."

It is February 14, the second day of Lent. This church, within walking distance of home, stirs memories of Mother, a devout Roman Catholic. After mass, the priest steps down from the altar. As he exits the sanctuary, a woman's voice rings out from a center pew.

"Today is Corrine Smith's birthday!"

As if on cue, the congregants begin to sing, "Happy birthday to you, happy birthday to you . . ." At the close of the stanza, they begin another, "May the good Lord bless you. . . ." I sing along, holding back tears. Valentine's Day was also the date of my mother's birth, and I find myself singing to her.

Afterward, on the way out, two black-suited men stand in the vestibule. Immediately outside the door is a hearse; funeral home ushers await the start of a burial mass.

One of them smiles. "It must be someone's birthday in there."

Yes, someone's birthday and someone else's death day. It is a day for remembering those with whom we are connected and those from whom we are separated.

God speaks in the parable of the prodigal son, and a voice of harmony arises. In this story, the younger son boldly asks for his share of his inheritance even before his father has died. Symbolic of God's generous sharing of worldly goods, the father indulges him. Inheritance in hand, the son sets off to a distant country and proceeds to squander all of the gift on "wild living." He becomes destitute, so much so that he hungers even for the pig slop in the fields where he tries to find work, but no one offers him a thing.

He returns home filled with sorrow and apology. In a tender gesture of forgiveness, his father not only runs to embrace this son but also throws him a party with the finest of accoutrements.

The older son, who has shown his father steadfast devotion and obedience, is a bit put off by the festivities, but the father reminds him that, since his inheritance is still intact, all that remains will be his. Additionally, there is reason to celebrate, for his brother was lost and now is found.

The parable speaks of our Creator's willingness to forgive, to reestablish harmony, and the celebration that's in store for the simple request of pardon.

The Quaker meetinghouse is sparse, for the most part undecorated. Rows of pews are arranged in a square and the center is empty, no altar, no minister or statues. The congregation seeks the Presence of the Divine in expectant silence. They listen. By whatever name we know the Truth—that of God, the Inward Light, Spirit, the Seed, the Light of Christ, the Still, Small Voice—the Quakers believe that it dwells within each of us. The endeavor, as Quaker George Fox described it, is to "walk cheerfully over all the world, answering that of God in everyone." And so the diversity of individual spiritual paths is embraced, as is the unity that transcends differences. The essence of worship is to remain open to the promptings of the Spirit. In silence, heads are bowed.

On this Sunday in Lent, it is good to settle into the quiet, eyes closed. It's safe to assume we are all seekers, each defining that as we may. Finally, a woman who is moved by the Spirit speaks of the connection she feels to the earth, of her gratitude for soil from which springtime is starting to blossom. Another marvels at how, because of modern technology, she is able to chat with and behold the image of her son who lives across the ocean. Again, silence. And then a man wonders aloud about the dichotomy between the promising growth of the season and the killings in a world fractured by war. He shares his struggle to make sense of a nation sending troops into countries where innocent people die. He asks for continued signs of a loving God and for the faith to trust.

Day after day, service after service, the voice I am hearing speaks of harmony, the quality for which I yearned with Mother, and the one I still seek. At another Lenten service, the Anglican priest speaks of a former cardinal from Buenos Aires who was installed this week as the new leader of the Roman Catholic Church. Pope Francis adopted the name recalling the asceticism of St. Francis of Assisi. The new papal leader once wrote the foreword to a book by a Jewish rabbi and referred to him as "my teacher."

The pastor notes that Bartholomew I, the spiritual leader of the world's Orthodox Christians, wrote a letter welcoming the new pope. He was among the 200,000 in attendance at the installation mass, the first time since 1054, when the Greek and Roman churches split, that the Orthodox leader had attended a papal investiture. As a symbol of common bonds between East and West, the Vatican decided that the Gospel during the mass would be chanted in Greek instead of Latin. The message, according to the minister, is this: It is time to heal the wound. Sometimes we carry things for too long. He approaches the pews dotted with worshippers, anoints foreheads, and one by one, says a prayer for each of us. It is a prayer of healing, one that asks help in setting aside differences and embracing a spirit of unity.

In Romans, Paul offers guidelines for living our faith day-to-day.

"Do not conform to the pattern of this world, but be transformed by the renewing of your mind. Then you will be able to test and approve what God's will is—his good, pleasing and perfect will.[85]

"Love must be sincere . . . Be devoted to one another in love. Honor one another above yourselves . . . Be joyful in hope, patient in affliction, faithful in prayer. Share with the Lord's people who are in need. Practice hospitality.

"Bless those who persecute you; bless and do not curse. Rejoice with those who rejoice; mourn with those who mourn. Live in harmony with one another."[86]

At a healing service on a Wednesday at noon, halfway through my Lenten pilgrimage, the congregation comprises one, just me. The small chapel is located in a former Sunday school room, a simple table as altar, two rows of folding chairs. Though the chapel is new, the building is familiar. Once longtime members of this church, Randy and I learned to know Jesus here. Eventually, the congregation, as well as the entire denomination, faced with theological challenges, became riddled with dissension.

The argument pitted those who interpret the letter of the law against those who embrace the spirit of the law. My husband and I disputed the stand that our pastor adamantly professed, and in spite of cherished bonds formed, we made the grueling decision to leave. Since then, I have come to realize that the beliefs that prompted us to move on—about embracing one another in spite of differences—were the very reasons that we should have stayed.

The God that I know is all about peace and unconditional love. Finding harmony—with each other and within ourselves—is a sacred calling. No matter how far we stray, thankfully God is God, and it is never too late—even for me with Mother, gone now but clearly resurrected by the Spirit. I do not think that she purposely pushed me away. As in her, there are traits in me—the worrying, the wandering, the pride, to name a few—that create distance. As with culinary attempts that always turn out a bit too tart, there comes a time to acknowledge the errors and change the recipe.

Now, for most of the service, the pastor, who is new since I belonged here, sits on one of the chairs not far from mine. He shares the readings; both of us stand for the Gospel. Instead of a sermon—"It would feel awkward," he admits—we meditate in silence. He moves closer to offer a prayer for healing in this place that once illuminated my need for it. The presence of the Holy Spirit is palpable, the sense of connection, the cleansing tears, the deep-felt comfort.

As the sole member of today's congregation, with head bowed, I remember the words of a clergyman long ago in this very place, who noted, "If you had been the only person in the world, Christ still would have died for you."

At a Mennonite church, the theme of the service—on the bulletin cover, on projection screens—is the very one I have been contemplating: "Listen." The reading from Psalm 42 begins, "As the deer pants for streams of water, so my soul pants for you, O God." The preacher notes that the first step in overcoming thirst is to recognize that we are thirsty. We must start by acknowledging our needs, our hurts, our pain.

A repetitive phrase throughout one of the readings is "God's unfailing love endures forever." Still, the Psalmist pleads, "Where are you, God? Have you forgotten me?"

"The problem is not that the Psalmist doesn't have faith," says the preacher. "The problem is that the unfailing love seems so far away."

He notes the healing power in being listened to. He cites a study that shows that the greatest predictor of success in young people is a connection to someone outside the family who listens to and respects them. He points out that God never intended to be our sole source of comfort, that God gave Adam a companion in Eve, that God gives each of us others on Earth to share love by listening.

Near the end of the service, parishioners are invited to turn to someone nearby and learn of the topic about which this neighbor would like to be heard. There is awkwardness throughout the congregation, some rumblings, whispers.

The woman in front of me turns and glances at me.

"How can I pray for you?" I ask her.

"Ummm, I don't have much," she says. "You go first. What would you like prayers about?"

"Reconciliation," I answer.

She takes my hands and prays softly, the loveliest of prayers. A sensation of release, of letting go, fills me. And I know that I have been heard.

How can we address a person who is no longer here on Earth, one whom there is no opportunity to meet face to face?

One time, after a book reading I'd delivered at a library, a woman wearing a cross approached me. Upon hearing my words about my final exchanges with my dying father, feelings of regret had welled up inside her over not having shared certain sentiments with her mother before she died.

"Do you think that if you expressed those thoughts to Jesus," I asked, "he would be willing to pass them along?"

Perhaps what I meant was something like this.

Dear Jesus, this may not sound like the most urgent of requests, but to me, as you know, it's important. I wonder if you might deliver a message to my mother? Would you remind her of the times when I was a little girl sitting on the ottoman in front of her living room chair? Together we watched television—*Lassie, The Ed Sullivan Show, The Twilight Zone, Dobie Gillis*—as she stroked my hair over and over, running her fingers through it. Like music that flutters from the strings of a harp, her touch filled me.

Neither of us spoke, but I can still feel her hands, sure yet tender, connecting us.

I don't know whether the woman in the library ever sent a message to her mother through Jesus, but that evening, as she considered it, a look of wonder and then relief settled upon her searching eyes.

"Immortal, invisible, God only wise . . . "
The Blue Hymnal lies open on the pew back in front of me, Number 423. In a beach town church that Randy and I are visiting, a crisp breeze wafts in through open windows. Voices rise like a group gift bearing unique signatures.
"Unresting, unhasting, and silent as light."
Silent as light. I close my eyes. The light is silent, as is God's presence; it is also powerful, embracing, and warm. Silence can be a summoning, a generous call to begin a search within. On the page, the silence prompted me to listen, to hear sacred voice, bringing Mother back again and unveiling light that otherwise might have gone unnoticed.

Maundy Thursday, the day commemorating the Last Supper, the commissioning of the bread and the wine. The Moravian Church where I slip into the pew for a four o'clock service is pristine, grand with simplicity. Congregants nod and smile, suggesting that on some level, they know me. It is the final communion until Easter when, before dawn, the

Moravian Trombone Choir will wander the streets through our quaint city heralding the resurrection. As old as the town itself, the tradition began when Lititz was formed by the Moravians in 1756. Musicians divide into groups, and head to different areas throughout the borough, stopping on street corners under lampposts. In joyous celebration, the song of trombones, trumpets, and tubas spreads the word of Easter. At some houses, faces appear at dark windows. At others, lights flicker on. At still others, sound sleepers continue to snooze, unaware of the concert being offered on the sidewalk outside. Year after year, my own eyes open at the sound. At first there is confusion, but then harmony stirs the soul, and the awakening is profound.

Now, in this historic church, I can hardly wait for Easter morning. The resurrection. My voice lifts in song, and I think of the hundreds of people—strangers, in most cases—with whom I've sung hymns and shared tenderness of spirit during this holiest of seasons. The music fills me full, breaking through silence, disparate voices coming together and rising, rising to a place where I can hear.

# *epilogue*

At the corner of Bleecker and Carmine Streets in the old Italian section of the West Village stands a patch of park—known as a piazza in the mother country—called Father Demo Square. My daughter and I sit on a bench here, an open bakery box on each of our laps. Pigeons strut along the macadam, pecking at infinitesimal gastronomic delights. A group of prospective NYU students, hands shading eyes from sun, listens to a guide singing the praises of Village nightlife. A buxom woman with long straggly hair is seated across the way, tossing morsels to the birds; her black T-shirt touts "I am Donald Trump's sex slave."

This sunny April afternoon has been delicious in every way. The tour we just finished meandered through Old Greenwich streets from one eatery to the next, where we savored the flavors; the sweet-smelling sauces, the generous portions reminiscent of Mother's kitchen. Pizza with homemade mozzarella from Joe's; risotto balls from Faicco's; cavolfiore at Palma; eggplant rollatini at Ristorante Rafele; cannoli from Paticceria Rocco. Afterward, we returned to the shops to buy homemade pasta, olive oil with basil, and the pastries that we are now devouring: a chocolate-dipped cookie that must be five inches in diameter, a pear-shaped French delicacy whose name I can't remember, a piece of strawberry shortcake, and a Napoleon. We indulge in the treats not because we are hungry—which is all but impos-

159

sible after the three-hour food tour—but because once we spied the endless pastry display case, we could not resist. For good or for bad, the two of us share the sweet-tooth gene.

So now here we are before traveling our separate ways, mother and daughter, breathing in the comfortable air—for which, it seems, the long, cold winter has forced us to wait forever—savoring the moments, breaking bread. There is an easy exchange about the day: the tour stops, the street musicians playing Motown in front of Amy's Bread, the nine-foot-wide row house once inhabited by Edna St. Vincent Millay.

A breeze lifts a wisp of long brown hair against sunglasses perched on top of my twenty-year-old's head. She bites into the cookie and closes her eyes, relishing. I wonder if someday she might return here, a mother herself with a daughter of her own. I can see the two of them side by side, perhaps on this very same bench, warmed by the sun. The mother holds pastry between finger and thumb, sinking her teeth into it, custard oozing from the sides. Both of them laugh, as the daughter reaches toward the one who brought her into the world and touches her cheek, gently brushing away the crumbs.

*If today you hear His voice,*
*harden not your hearts.*

Psalm 95:7–8

# questions for reflection & discussion

1. According to Romans 8:25, "We are hoping for something we do not have yet, and we are waiting for it patiently." What are you hoping for, waiting for, praying for?

2. Think back. Who are the people who influenced you, the members of your discernment committee? Try to recall those who encouraged you, as well as those who tested your convictions. Through retroactive listening, in what ways do you now hear the Spirit's voice?

3. How would you answer this question: How does faith play a role in my vocation?

4. Consider what turns your life has taken that made you stray from the paths you had in mind. Try to pinpoint the presence of the Holy Spirit before, during, or after life's detours and challenges.

5. What are the worries that prevent God's voice from reaching you? How would your days be different if you trusted the promise of a God who holds your right hand and says, "Do not fear: I will help you?" (Isaiah 41:13)

6. Think about what you might subtract from your life—attitudes, activities, distractions—to get more in sync with a voice of peace.

7. Meditate on the verse "For where your treasure is, there your heart will be also." What does this mean to you in terms of your own priorities?

8. What talents do you have that you see as expressions of God's love? In what ways do your special gifts make a giver of you? In what ways do they help you to receive?

9. When you think of the unfathomable character of life—or unexpected moments of grace—as divine gift, what experiences come to mind?

10. What commitments are needed for you to live a life of listening and learning to follow an inner spiritual voice?

# With deepest gratitude

to those who offered support and encouragement,
to those who provided much-needed space,
to those who were generous with their expertise, and
to those who were and are with me in spirit.

*The author and her mother, 1951.*

**Jan Groft** is the author of a memoir, *Riding the Dog*, and the award-winning book *As We Grieve*. She lives and writes in Lancaster County, Pennsylvania. You are invited to visit her at jangroft.com and facebook.com/JanGroftAuthor.

**Josephine C. Coco** (1914–2006) was the mother of five daughters, the grandmother of twelve, the great-grandmother of eighteen, and the great-great-grandmother of an ever-increasing number, many of whom she never met. The recipes featured in *Artichokes & City Chicken* represent her endeavors to nurture and nourish generations of a growing breed.

# *notes*

## Preface

1   Judith Viorst, *Necessary Losses* (New York: Ballantine Books, 1986), 19
2   Viorst, 21–22
3   Ann Tyler, *Dinner at the Homesick Restaurant* (New York: Random House, 1982), 125

## Chapter One: If a Tree Falls in the Forest

4   Structured Living was the name of the dementia wing of the retirement community where my mother lived.
5   Oswald Chambers, *My Utmost for His Highest*, ed. James G. Reimann (Grand Rapids, MI: Discovery House Publishers, 1992), October 11
6   Stephen Levine, *Unattended Sorrow* (Emmaus, PA: Rodale, Inc., 2005), 92
7   John 11:21; John 11:32
8   John 11:40
9   John 11:35
10  Matthew 27:46
11  Proverbs 2:10–11
12  Catherine Marshall, *Adventures in Prayer* (Old Tappan, NJ: Chosen Books, 1975), 86

13  John 1:23

14  Rachel Simon, *The Writer's Survival Guide* (Cincinnati, OH: Story Press, 1997), 117–118

15  Max Lucado, *Experiencing the Heart of Jesus* (Nashville, TN: Thomas Nelson, Inc., 2003), 29

16  Revelation 1:15

17  *The Random House College Dictionary*, Revised Edition, s.v. "voice"

18  Isaiah 30:21

19  Psalm 19:3

20  Hebrews 11:13

21  Levine, 60

22  1 Samuel 3:9

**Chapter Two: Waiting**

23  Milton Mayeroff, *On Caring* (New York, NY: HarperCollins, 1971), 70

24  Eugene H. Peterson, *The Message: The Bible in Contemporary Language* (Colorado Springs, CO: Alive Communications, 2005), Romans 8:25

25  Whitney T. Kuniholm, *The Essential Bible Guide* (Colorado: Shaw Books, 2003), 180

26  Ibid. 183

27  Isaiah 30:18

28  Mark E. Thibodeaux, SJ, *God's Voice Within: The Ignatian Way to Discover God's Will* (Chicago: Loyola Press, 2010), 53

29  John 1:14

30 Richard Weissbound, *The Parents We Mean to Be* (New York: Houghton Mifflin Harcourt Publishing, 2009), 7

31 Ibid. 41

32 Frederick Buechner, *Wishful Thinking: A Seeker's ABC* (San Francisco: Harper San Francisco, 2003), 119

33 Isaiah 61:10

## Chapter Three: The Discernment Committee

34 Thibodeaux, 73

35 www.amazon.com/Council-Dads-Family-Friend-ship-Learning/dp/006177877X/ref=sr_1_1?ie=UT-F8&qid=1441290187&sr=8-1&keywords=Councils-Dads-Family-Learning

## Chapter Four: Subtracting

36 Psalm 119:37

37 1 Corinthians 14:33

38 Mayeroff, 87

39 Matthew 6:21

40 Peterson, Matthew 6:19-21

41 Matthew 19:24

42 Matthew 22:37

43 Matthew 22:39

44 Lamentations 1:5

45 Chambers, July 4

46 John 14:27

47 Luke 12:25

48  Isaiah 41:13

49  Matthew 6:34

50  Chambers, June 2

51  Jeremiah 29:11

52  Joshua 1:9


## Chapter Five: Mattering

53  Howard Long, "Howard's Thoughts," September 3, 2012.
    Bible+1 [Mobile Application Software], Just1word,Inc.

54  Chambers, October 16

55  Barbara Brown Taylor. *An Altar in the World* (New York:
    HarperCollins, 2009), 110–111

56  2 Corinthians 1:3–5

57  Harold S. Kushner, *Living a Life That Matters* (New York:
    Random House, 2001), 6


## Chapter Six: Wandering & Watching

58  Matthew 14:29-31

59  Kuniholm, 201

60  H. E. Shepherd, "The History of Coincide and Co-
    incidence," *The American Journal of Philology*, Vol. I,
    No. 3 (1880), (Johns Hopkins University Press, DOI:
    10.2307/287556), 271-276, www.jstor.org/stable/287556

61  James Redfield and Carol Adrienne, *The Celestine Prophecy:
    An Experiential Guide* (New York: Warner Books, 1995), 3

62  James 1:4

63 Frederick Buechner, *Telling Secrets* (New York: HarperCollins, 1991), 1

64 2 Corinthians 12:10

## Chapter Seven: The Unfathomable Character of Life

65 Eve Joseph, "Yellow Taxi." *At the End of Life.* Lee Gutkind, ed. (Pittsburgh: Creative Nonfiction Books, 2012), 56

66 Mayeroff, 92–93

67 Acts 3:15

68 Matthew 5:13–14

69 John 10:14–15

70 1 John 3:1

71 Psalm 17:8

72 Peterson, Matthew 10:20

## Chapter Eight: Drinking the Water

73 James 4:8

74 *The Random House College Dictionary*, Revised Edition, s.v. "immersion"

75 Jeremiah 2:13

76 Psalm 36:9

77 Isaiah 55:1

78 Chambers, July 28

79 Philippians 4:7

80 1 Corinthians 13:1

81 1 Corinthians 13:4–7

## Chapter Nine: The Moravian Trombone Choir